dear mary

Books by Sarah Jakes

Colliding With Destiny
Lost and Found
Dear Mary

dear mary

Lessons From the Mother
of Jesus for the Modern Mom

SARAH JAKES

BETHANYHOUSE
a division of Baker Publishing Group
Minneapolis, Minnesota

Published by Bethany House Publishers
11400 Hampshire Avenue South
Bloomington, Minnesota 55438
www.bethanyhouse.com

Bethany House Publishers is a division of
Baker Publishing Group, Grand Rapids, Michigan

Paperback edition published 2017
978-0-7642-1911-5

Printed in the United States of America

The Library of Congress has cataloged the hardcover edition as follows:
Jakes, Sarah.
        Dear Mary : lessons from the mother of Jesus for the modern mom / Sarah
    Jakes.
            pages cm
        Summary: "Written in the form of letters to Mary, the mother of Jesus, this book offers reflections on her remarkable life and encouragement to moms and women of faith today"— Provided by publisher.
        ISBN 978-0-7642-1212-3 (cloth : alk. paper)
        1. Motherhood—Religious aspects—Christianity. 2. Mothers—Religious life. 3. Mary, Blessed Virgin, Saint—Miscellanea. I. Title.
    BV4529.18.J34 2015
    248.8'431—dc23   2015015886

Cover design by Gearbox
Cover photography by Will Sterling

Author is represented by Dupree/Miller & Associates

17   18   19   20   21   22   23   7   6   5   4   3   2   1

contents

introduction

by Cora Jakes-Coleman

*D*ear Mary,

As mothers, we have difficulty with every new struggle, level, and storm our children go through, whether it's starting school, going off to college, battling addiction, teen pregnancy, adoption, and the list goes on. In addition to being challenging, walking our children through these stages often requires a huge sacrifice on our part. As I think about your example as a mother, I am amazed by the sacrifices you made for the betterment of the world. As I think of your story, and your Son's story, I am in awe of your ability to trust God without doubt, hesitation, or resistance—never once worrying about what anyone might say, including Joseph.

You accepted God's call, probably not even considering the pain, agony, and sacrifice required. Your story empowers mothers, while also challenging us to believe God in ways that we never have before. As a mother myself, I wonder how hard it was for you to accept this call and trust God. I wonder if modern-day mothers would have accepted the call at all, or would we have missed our opportunity to know you because of our fear of the unknown? I wonder if we would have heard the angel's voice, or would we have been watching television, listening to music, always remaining distracted by the things of the world—simply busy establishing our own plans?

I can only imagine how hard it must have been as a young woman to give up your dreams and desires for God's plan. I can only imagine how hard it must have been to carry a child knowing that one day He would have to go through unbelievable pain and agony for your sake. As a mother, it had to be extremely difficult to sacrifice yourself so that your child could accomplish His purpose on earth. As a mother who fought to be a mother, I admire your ability to be so self-sacrificing. You opened your body to receive a gift that you would later have to give to the world.

Your ability to allow God to bless you with something indescribable later gave us the ability to receive and understand indescribable blessings. As women, we now seek the impossible because you had the faith to birth the One who makes all things possible in an impossible way. A mother's love is indescribable, but a mother's sacrifice is priceless. You lovingly raised your child, preparing Him for His assignment of bringing salvation to the world, knowing fully that it would break your heart.

You, Mary, defied all odds, and fought a fight that no mother will ever be able to match. You, Mary, stood for the broken person, the hurting person, the lost person, and you produced salvation through yourself, for yourself and for the world. Did you know that your baby boy would save you? Did you know that the life you gave to Him, He would turn around and give back to you? Did you know that you would birth faith for the faithless and healing for the broken? Did you truly know what it meant when the angel said you would give birth to Emmanuel? Did you know that you would also sacrifice your heart as a mother so that your Son could give His heart to the world?

What an amazing story, that you would give your body so that your Son could give His body as a living sacrifice. You are not just a mother, but a mother that birthed a gift for all. I would later develop the desire and the dream of becoming a mother to a son because of your sacrifice. Mary, because of your sacrifice, I am determined to fight for my promise of a child.

You, Mary, are the mother who made every other mother possible. You are the mother who made every fight possible. You are the mother who birthed salvation into the world because you accepted a gift that anyone else would have turned away. Mary, through you, we would develop hope and come to understand that sometimes our promises are only made manifest through the sacrifices of our hearts.

A mother's love is indescribable, but a mother's sacrifice is priceless.

Mary, we applaud you as the mother who won—and lost. We applaud you as the mother who birthed greatness so that we could receive the promise of His great reward and, yes, even our own greatness.

Dear Mary, thank you for accepting the call. Mary, you are what a mother is. You are what a mother does, and you are what every mother should strive to be. You taught us that mothering is not about us, but rather about guiding and nurturing our children so they are able to walk in God's chosen purpose for their lives. Mary, you taught us how to be a mother, and for that lesson we applaud you.

Cora Jakes-Coleman

*D*ear Mothers,

I don't think there is a group that compares themselves to each other more than mothers. The quest for guidance and approval leaves us observing the steps and patterns of motherhood very closely. One mother I've studied can be found beginning her journey in the New Testament.

The life of Mary has been so significant for me because history reveals that she was a teenage mother. Certainly the times were much different then, and teen pregnancy didn't have the same stigma it does now. However, there was something about a young girl being trusted with life that made me want to examine how she was able to survive mental, emotional, and physical attacks. I imagined that once the news of God's impregnating her began to circulate, she was called crazy and made to become an outcast. There is no woman in the Bible more fitting to give insight on becoming a mother under extraordinary circumstances than Mary.

When my children came to an age when they were no longer oohing and ahhing in baby talk, I realized they were copying what they saw in me. My son has many of my mannerisms and has inherited my sense of humor. My daughter has much of my charisma and emulates my clothing style. I never sat them down and told them which parts of my personality to take. They'd learned more from what I didn't

11

say than any words I ever uttered. So when the time came to write this book for us, you and me, I knew the clues to the mentality of Mary would reside in the actions of Christ.

Of course, there would come a time when Christ was able to access God for himself, but through His infancy Mary and Joseph were entrusted to raise Him back to God. Imagine how easy it would have been to raise Him with no knowledge of the mandate on His life. Perhaps He would have been raised "normally" and would have never discovered the gifting inside of Him. There was a courageous commitment to share truth, whether or not it would be universally accepted. That same courage dwelled in Christ as He faced the Pharisees and converted the Gentiles. That courage exists in me. It exists in you. It exists in our children.

Sarah Jakes

1

anxious and pregnant

"Blessed is she who has believed that the
Lord would fulfill his promises to her!"

Luke 1:45

*D*ear Mary,

You know better than anyone that the gift of life is a miracle. In your case, an angel visited you, and instantaneously you were pregnant by the Holy Spirit. There's not a womb before you or since that can contend with that. But that doesn't downplay the biological miracle of pregnancy. A woman is born with one to two million eggs in her body. As a woman ages, those eggs begin to die off and decrease. The process of one of those eggs making contact with a man's sperm can only be described as a phenomenon.

Once a month a woman's ovary releases an egg. A man's sperm must fertilize that egg, or it will be discarded through her menstrual cycle. A man releases at least forty million sperm each time he ejaculates, yet only one will have the strength to travel through a woman's reproductive system and make contact with the egg. All of this must take place within twenty-four hours of the egg's release from the ovary, before the egg becomes unviable. From there the fertilized egg must travel to the woman's uterus, implant in the uterine wall, and then begin a nine-month process of development.

In a world inundated with adorable baby faces, tiny little clothes, and infant giggles, it can be easy to lose sight of the miraculous journey that must take place from conception to parenting. As a mother of two and stepmother to three, it doesn't escape me how humbling the gift of motherhood is. There's no way to fully explain the state of awe a woman finds herself in when she learns her body will transform a cluster of cells into a person. There are some questions that are universal regardless of your age, socioeconomic level, or marital status.

Is my body strong enough to handle this? Should I rest or push myself to continue like normal? What will the baby look like? When will I feel it kick? Who do I tell first? Should I wait to tell at all? How will my family react? Will my mother try to take over? Will this baby bridge the divide between my sister and me? How do I choose a doctor? Will the hospital nurses be nice? Baby names? Boy or girl? Baby shower?

Will I be prepared to handle all that lies ahead?

There are a million questions forming in the minds of expectant mothers. Swimming in a sea of excitement, anxiety, joy, fear, hope, and stress is a woman who knows that life has forever changed, but who can't pinpoint exactly when it will all begin. Most women begin to think of family or friends who've recently given birth or are a few months ahead of them in pregnancy. Their sisterhood of motherhood is a gift that only those brave enough to be vulnerable fully understand. There's much wisdom to be gleaned simply by having someone who understands exactly where you've been and what you're going through.

After experiencing my own pregnancies and sea of questions, I feel I understand you a bit better. Your sisterhood in motherhood was your cousin Elizabeth. As soon as you came to visit her after learning the news of your pregnancy, the baby inside her womb leaped. Before you could even begin to express to her your reaction, she described how blessed you would be because you believed the Lord would fulfill His promises to you.

Initially, I didn't understand why it would be so difficult for you to believe; after all, an angel appeared to deliver your news. It would seem quite easy to believe after an experience like that. This just goes to show how much I've taken for granted the miracle of pregnancy. The reality is that much of the second-guessing women experience upon learning of their pregnancy is rooted in disbelief. Unsure of our ability to carry and nurture, we begin weighing all the possible mistakes or misfortune that we could experience. Yet you showed such courage and faith to trust that God would not set a miracle in motion without a plan for completion. What strength one must possess to see the answers to their questions by faith! For every hurdle, jungle, and mountain the trail of motherhood presents for us, God has made a provision that will allow our spirits to prosper in hope.

I certainly wish I could have found those words when I ended my call with my friend Misty two months ago. She was beginning to feel like it would take more than a miracle to adjust to becoming a mom again.

I can remember exactly what I was doing when I found out. She called me from her office at the firm where she works. Whispering into the receiver so that she couldn't be overheard, she asked, "What's your calendar like in April?"

"Misty, I don't even know what I'm eating for lunch today. I definitely don't know what I'm doing months from now," I replied.

She chuckled at my response before dropping the bomb, "Well, will you come visit me at the hospital? I'm going to have a baby. I hear the cafeteria has great food!"

Surprised at the announcement, I immediately screamed my congratulations at the top of my lungs. "WE'RE HAVING A BABY!!!" I yelled. After my exclamation, all I could hear was her laughing. I imagined her clamoring for buttons to turn the volume down on her office line while she giggled through the laundry list of questions I had: "How far along are you? When did you find out? What are you hoping for, and don't just give me the 'healthy baby' line!" One-by-one in rapid-fire style, I asked her everything that came to mind.

Just as quickly she replied: "About five weeks. This morning. You're the first person I called. A girl."

After covering baby names and allowing me a ten-minute monologue expressing my envy that her stomach would no longer be confined by Spanx, girdles, and other control-top devices, we ended our call. I was so happy for her!

We grew up in church. We were taught to believe that babies are a blessing. Sure, there were complicated instances of new life coming into the world. Many a woman, like me, first held her child with no ring on her finger, and confused that sentiment a bit. On one hand, every life is a gift from God, but I believe it became difficult not to allow the sin to overcloud the joy. Too often we see the baby thrown out with the baby water. Luckily for Misty, she wouldn't have to face any of those predicaments. She was doing things the "right" way.

I believe that's why I was so surprised when I hung up from our latest call. She called me moments after I'd finished working out at the gym. I placed the phone on mute while I caught my breath and listened to my friend confide her secret fears to me. "Honestly, it's hard to be excited about the baby these days. . . ."

I couldn't imagine what worries she had. Before she could finish her sentence, I began searching for any reason she should be disappointed or afraid. This would be baby number four for her, so she'd be pretty well prepared for what to expect. Misty was just about to celebrate her fifteen-year wedding anniversary. She wouldn't be worrying about the judgment that can come with being a single mother. I ran scenario after scenario through my head, and all I could see was a white picket fence.

When my mind stopped racing long enough to ask her what her concerns were, it all came out. Misty was having a hard time smiling about the baby when she was already consumed with worry about providing for the mouths outside of her tummy. They would have to find somewhere new to live, or make do with the limited space in their home. Her husband had lost his job about a year earlier, and finding consistent income proved to require more patience than either of them anticipated. She told me that she was doing the best she possibly could to be optimistic, but the last week had been particularly difficult to find the rainbow in the midst of her storm.

I'm hardly ever at a loss for words, but I truly didn't know what to tell her. I pacified her with the age-old responses I'm sure she was prepared to hear: "It'll all work out. Everything will be okay!" I continued to spew out every cliché I could find until she was the one convincing me that everything would work out. When we hung up the phone, I couldn't help but ask God why there was no clear formula to peace. While my friend, for all intents and purposes, did things the "right" way, she still had obstacles to face.

I was seeing her life through my insecurities. I assumed that, because she didn't have the struggles I was familiar with, she didn't struggle at all. We miss the opportunity to be compassionate when we confine people to our own experiences. Misty helped me to realize that we aren't just puzzle pieces looking to create the perfect picture. We're souls seeking the strength to accept—in spite of how we've been bent and curved—that our life still has purpose.

Life is difficult when you have an audience to watch you battle, but it's dangerous when you have an internal battle no one can witness. My life was difficult as a young teen mom. All I desired was to get married so that I wouldn't feel the haunting judgment from others. I couldn't pretend everything was okay, because the evidence of life had already dispelled that myth.

What do you do when you have a life someone else would envy, but you can't bear to admit that it's not as easy as it looks? It's hard to not feel the distress that comes with bringing a life into the world when you consider the potential calamity he or she will have to face. We are expected to create an environment where our children can grow and flourish under our care. But often we're too stifled by our own insecurities to allow them any room to grow. Having given up on ourselves, our task becomes to at minimum provide better for them than we had for ourselves.

We miss the opportunity to be compassionate when we confine people to our own experiences.

I will never forget visiting my mother in the middle of a difficult time in my first marriage. I hadn't said a word, but when my mother saw my face and then peered into the eyes of my daughter, she knew something was wrong. At that time she warned me that if I didn't come out of my depression, I was going to take my daughter into it with me. My daughter, Makenzie, was emulating the expressions of my pain—no matter how well I thought I was doing at shielding her. The reality is, you can't constantly be around someone without their seeing every part of you, even the parts that still hurt.

If you do not confront your pain, you will spread it. My dear friend was giving me the opportunity to fight with her, but I couldn't see beyond my own scars. When she mentioned her frustrations, I felt my own issues leap, but I didn't tell her that. Our situations were very different. I didn't feel my experiences would be relatable to her. I wanted to give Misty some type of confirmation that even though things looked problematic on paper, God would work things out. I just didn't believe sharing what happened on the inside of *me* would help her. I knew reviving her faith wasn't about just her but about the lives observing her as well

We can't be faithless and raise faithful children.

We can't be faithless and raise faithful children.

Mary, when Gabriel informed you that God had chosen you to carry His Son, He also revealed that your cousin Elizabeth was expecting as well. Though you were just receiving the news, she was already six months pregnant. Sometimes those closest to us face obstacles before we do so that we can learn from them. We can't be ashamed to share our lessons even though we know everyone's test will be different. I felt guilty. I wanted to give Misty a reason to believe, but I couldn't see beyond my own past.

You could've felt bitterness that Elizabeth was already married when she conceived. Elizabeth could've envied you that she wasn't chosen to give birth to Christ. Elizabeth was older and had been barren. You were young and a virgin. Gabriel visited you to inform you of your pregnancy, but he had visited Elizabeth's husband to deliver their news. Amid all the similarities, there were these small but significant differences. Still, your faith to believe was the divine bond that held you together.

Gabriel used Elizabeth's pregnancy to underscore to you that nothing is impossible with God (see Luke 1:37). Your salutation to Elizabeth after learning the news of your future child filled her with the Holy Spirit (see Luke 1:41). There was no way you could know what happened on the inside of her unless she was willing to be vulnerable enough to share it with you. You never would have suspected that your words filled her with joy until she told you. The transparency in your friendship afforded you the opportunity to confirm one another's faith.

Anxiety magnifies the size of our obstacles, but faith gives us the power to rise above our struggles.

That's what I want to do with Misty. That's all I desire to do with my children. I want my little ones to enjoy seeing their fears in the rearview mirror of their destiny. One day my children will realize that anxiety magnifies the size of our obstacles, but faith gives us the power to rise above our struggles. Love builds a tunnel from one soul to another. We must be careful what we let in and sure about what we release. When we feel those we are connected to are allowing fear into their hearts, we can combat it by allowing more faith, love, and hope to gush through our channel. Our fears can drown in the flood of our promise, but we must be willing to believe. We can't become like those who choose to let fear dilute the power of their promise.

The leap in my womb may be the confirmation someone else needs that she can believe. More than cliché reassurances of a better tomorrow, through transparency we offer our scars as evidence of survival.

Sharing those imperfections with your children can be very scary. One day I'll ask you how you received the courage to tell Jesus your own truth, but until then, I want to thank you for sharing your moment with another believing woman. Elizabeth answered your question of "Why me?" with one simple answer: Because you believed.

If we are wise, we will build children with only the bricks God hands us, not the rocks life has thrown at us.

I am learning that many of the rights and wrongs of motherhood come down to what we believe to be true. If we are wise, we will build children with only the bricks God hands us, not the rocks life has thrown at us. We will choose to believe God. No statistic, employer, bank statement, or matter of paternity can rob us of our promise. Unless we choose to believe it can.

We can't tell our children how to believe. We can only demonstrate how. I once believed in fear. I even believed in pain. I began to doubt love. I saw my hope slipping away, but then I was reminded that I had little eyes watching and small hearts in my hands. I may not be the best math tutor they'll ever have. I can't guarantee each meal will be a hit. But I pray each day that I will model a walk of faith for them and all those with whom I'm connected.

2

i'm still learning

As you do not know the path of the wind,
or how the body is formed in a mother's
womb, so you cannot understand the work
of God, the Maker of all things.

Ecclesiastes 11:5

*D*ear Mary,

I have two children, a son, Malachi, and a daughter, Makenzie. The circumstances surrounding their births is a book in itself. Literally, I wrote a memoir, *Lost and Found*, which recounts the journey that led to their introductions into the world. To be honest, I didn't feel at my best when I had either of them. At the time they were born, I was completely unsure of who I was or what potential existed inside of me. I've always felt like an ordinary girl in an extraordinary world. I could see purpose in every existence but my own. Their lives gave mine meaning.

My journey of becoming comfortable in my own skin hasn't been easy. I often wonder how I survived many of the choices I made. I know that I repeatedly and intentionally put myself in harm's way. It took me some time to even embrace that truth. Somehow, in spite of all the things I knew, I chose to hurt when I could have healed. Few things urge you to examine your life like parenting. We often fear that we may not be prepared to handle what we see reflected in the eyes of those we bring into the world. I know with certainty that I self-inflicted many of the wounds that are now scars on my heart, but each of them came with a valuable lesson. They also came with the perfect prescription and dosage for the pain.

At seven pounds and nine ounces, my first dose of unconditional love came in the form of Malachi Alexander. I remember watching as my young body began to transform for his entrance into the world. Long before I felt him kick or even took a test, I noticed my breasts begin to swell. It didn't take long before I started noticing other changes in my body. I noticed small bumps of acne forming on my back. Meanwhile, my once oily teenage face was now extremely dry. I had sporadic nosebleeds. It wasn't until my first trip to the doctor's office that I realized these seemingly unrelated issues were all symptoms of my recently discovered pregnancy.

Medicine has made quite a few advancements since you were with child. Every week of a woman's pregnancy has been calculated to an exact science. From the moment of conception, the female body begins to expand for the life that will occupy her womb for the next nine months. The gestational traits of pregnancy have many similarities, but every woman has a unique experience that cannot be scientifically analyzed or medically explained. The precise moment you fall completely in love with someone you've never met cannot be computed.

On Mother's Day of 2002 my older sister, Cora, my mother, and I went on a "staycation." We packed a bag and found a quiet room on the other side of town. Malachi was due just a few short months from then in October. Uninterested in the fine cuisine offered by the hotel restaurant, we enjoyed an assortment of items from the room service children's menu. Over a feast of chicken tenders, spaghetti, hamburgers, cookies, and ice cream, we indulged until we couldn't take another bite. Then, when we could no longer fight our sleep, we all piled into the king-sized bed and drifted into sweet dreams.

The next morning, we slowly began to toss and turn until we fully awakened. My mother softly said my name, and my eyes cracked open. Her voice has always been rich, smooth, and warm like velvet. With a whisper she can awaken any of her five children from their deepest slumber. "The baby was moving all night," she said. I can't imagine those were words she thought she'd ever be telling her thirteen-year-old daughter.

My first reaction was to apologize. I knew that processing my teenage pregnancy and anticipating the journey ahead of me had not been easy on my parents. I didn't want to create any unnecessary reminders, since I knew my growing belly was just weeks from becoming undeniable. I didn't apologize, though, because my second reaction came just as quickly as the first: *My baby is moving!*

The small flutters in my abdomen that I'd attributed to pregnancy indigestion were the actual flutters of my son flipping in my womb. Suddenly, it all became real. I would be responsible for another life. We were sharing the same body for the next few months. Everything I ate I would share with him. The positions I could sleep in would be determined by what was comfortable for him. My son's livelihood in the womb was solely dependent upon my ability to take care of myself. Once I gave birth, those responsibilities would shift and his livelihood would depend solely on my ability to physically care for and protect him. That thought was scarier than his being inside of me. At least I was a barrier between him and the many elements of the outside world. What if I didn't know exactly what to do with him when he came out?

I can't imagine being in your shoes, Mary. But trust me, I've tried to fathom what it would be like to have an angel appear to me and declare I'd been chosen to carry the Son of God. Each time, my reaction varies from hours of speechlessness to a gazillion questions at once to a list of more suitable candidates.

Did you ever wonder how everything was going to work? Would labor still hurt? Would angels deliver His food? Would He truly understand just how much you love Him? Not much is known about your life before Christ. Were you, like me, a heart still searching for ultimate significance and purpose in life? Was your esteem high enough to drown out fear and insecurities? Mine wasn't.

My son was, and continues to be, the flood of love that keeps me afloat in my most difficult days. I knew that God was assigning an angel to me. I wasn't sure exactly what He was saving me from, but I knew my son's life carried a message. Before I ever became pregnant, when my idealistic preteen self would daydream of someday wedding colors and baby names, I had never considered giving my child a name with religious meaning. A part of me didn't want to bestow a spiritual name that a child may not have the desire to live up to. I grew up in church, but I hadn't learned that we're all facing internal battles because we're fully human but were created in the image of God. I didn't recognize the tension this creates. After I became pregnant, what I came to know for sure was that, in spite of all the human frailties that led to his entrance into the world, I needed my son to remember that he was created in the image of God. So I decided to name him Malachi, messenger of God. I was admitted into the hospital on Wednesday, October 2, 2002, at 7:00 p.m. Malachi was born a full twenty-six hours later at 9:03 p.m. His life hasn't stopped speaking yet!

When labor shifted to delivery, delivery to recovery, and recovery back to my upstairs bedroom in my parents' home, I began to plan. Envisioning our future and making the best of our present had my undivided attention. I was determined to prove that I could care for us both. All while a woman's body is being prepared for the physical act of giving birth, her heart is being prepared for the many labors of love, fear, excitement, and joy that is motherhood. Each labor carries with it a delivery of faith to help make the next contraction easier to bear. Moments of inexpressible promise make every struggle worth the hope we find in the eyes of our babies. I didn't think it was possible for my heart to hold any more love.

Each labor carries with it a delivery of faith to help make the next contraction easier to bear.

I was wrong.

Seven years later, weighing in at eight pounds and eleven ounces, my daughter, Makenzie, came into the world. I must admit I thought I would be a veteran my second time around. I assumed that because my body had already transformed to carry life once before, things would be easier. That notion was dispelled seven weeks into my first trimester. At the emergency room of our local hospital, I was diagnosed with a kidney infection. Although the doctor said it wasn't related to my pregnancy at all, I had a sneaking suspicion he was wrong. It wasn't until my third emergency room visit that the doctor began to consider that there could be a correlation between the chronic kidney infection and the beautiful life inside of me.

I can tell you after five years of experiencing the joy that is Makenzie Ann's presence, those infections were a bit of foreshadowing. Much like the pregnancy that allowed her to make a debut into the world, her life has stretched and pulled so much out of me. Her life inspired me to look at the soul infections that existed in my heart and controlled my actions. It becomes increasingly clear with each passing moment that she is as headstrong, confident, and resilient as her mother. While those qualities are among the many things I love about her, they are also the qualities that keep me in prayer. She has the energy and creativity to do whatever she dreams. On the list of my prayer priorities is that I'm able to create an environment that incubates those qualities for God's ultimate purpose for her life.

I hope to teach her the beauty and strength of vulnerability. It is my prayer that she never suffers because she was too afraid to ask for help. I see her jump up from scrapes and bruises so quickly that she doesn't allow herself the opportunity to truly confess the pain she is experiencing. I know that trait is inherited, but I pray my life teaches her the lesson I've learned to grow the most confident in: You don't have to pretend life doesn't hurt.

You don't have to pretend life doesn't hurt.

As vibrant as the happiness and joy that surrounds us are, there is another element that we must learn to respect, navigate, and embrace: pain. Our pain creates the valley that allows our hope to spring. My Makenzie helped me discover my own reservoir of potential. One of the missions I hold most near to my heart is my responsibility to help her discover and protect the force she is—spunky, charming, and intelligent. I'm anxiously awaiting the day that she realizes how great a gift she is to the world and to me.

My final destination in life is yet being revealed, but I am committed to holding the hands of my children and protecting their hearts through it all. I must admit I wish they came with a forecast of things to expect and tips on how to weather each day. The advancement of science has allowed us to create hypothetical observations of bodily development, but nothing allows us a glimpse inside the thoughts and hearts of our children.

It is possible to endure labor without the aid of pain management, but raising children without faith guarantees more suffering than necessary. Whether a woman acquires the strength necessary to rise to the challenge of motherhood or finds herself too inadequate to care for another person, we never stop holding our children in our hearts. We can hold tight or let go, but we can never erase the impression of added life that was once inside of us. The greatest gift we can offer our children is the patience to maximize our faith in the face of the mysterious.

That's not to say that our process will be without flaws, but we can be diligent in our effort to explore God's work in our lives. Resisting the temptation to take our lives into our own hands and rush His construction will yield great reward. The fear of the unknown in parenting can entice us into planning every dimension of our child's life. We create a list of all the things they must become in order for us to be satisfied with a job well done. That level of precaution teaches our children to rely too heavily on their own ability and not nearly enough on God. We're too human to offer perfection, but we can create upbringings where devotion to God can flourish and provide nutrients to our children as they develop. It is impossible to teach a faith we do not live, nor can we exemplify unconditional love if we do not trust—lest we give them skewed examples. We must shelter our faith with the same fervor we guard our children.

There are many women who had their children in idyllic situations—and many more who found themselves, like us, pregnant outside of the accepted societal norm. You know firsthand, Mary, how difficult circumstances can compound the pains of labor and delivery. It wasn't enough that you had to endure the scandalous shame of losing your good reputation and disappointing your confused fiancé, but you also had to traipse across the countryside for a census. I can't imagine riding miles and miles on the back of a donkey in my last trimester! And then to arrive there and find that there's not even a tiny room in the back of any Bethlehem inn? But you made do and found a cradle for your baby in a barn, surrounded by angels and shepherds.

We can never erase the impression of added life that was once inside of us.

History has done a phenomenal job of teaching us to expect the unexpected. The formula for happiness and success has a composition as unique as DNA. It doesn't matter how a child is brought into the world; God can still use that life for His glory.

Mary, I'm not sure how you managed to overcome the self-defeating thoughts that fear implants in us. I dare not suggest that every day was easy for you, but I am certain that I am a beneficiary and student of your faith. I pray that I can learn to focus on God's promise for our lives even when confronted with adversity. I hope that I will never become so conflicted that I cease to trust God and only count on my own power. I have no desire to raise these children if I can't offer them back to Him. My heart is in constant search for the divine presence of God as I filter my love for my children with His grace.

Within a week of delivering each of my children, I began to miss some of the joys that come with pregnancy. I will never experience another childbirth that produces the same child, but life promises contractions of the

It doesn't matter how a child is brought into the world; God can still use that life for His glory.

soul that I must endure so that they may live. There is no way of knowing when the next contraction is coming or the severity it will bring, but I trust that I am prepared to survive the labor of love that is motherhood. With your example, Mary, I trust that I can be resourceful and uncomplaining when things don't go as planned and my inn is full. I hope I have your patience and grace to handle life's unexpected complications.

3

we have daddy issues

Abraham took the wood for the burnt offering and placed it on his son Isaac, and he himself carried the fire and the knife. As the two of them went on together, Isaac spoke up and said to his father Abraham, "Father?"

"Yes, my son?" Abraham replied.

"The fire and wood are here," Isaac said, "but where is the lamb for the burnt offering?"

Abraham answered, "God himself will provide the lamb for the burnt offering, my son."

Genesis 22:6–8

*D*ear Mary,

The Old Testament Scripture holds a timeless tale of righteousness and unparalleled faith in the life of Abraham. You don't have to be a theologian to know the Genesis 22 story of God telling Abraham to bind his son Isaac on an altar as a sacrifice to God. Seconds before he would bring the sword down and end his son's life, an angel appeared, stopping him. Abraham's faith was commended, and a nearby ram was used as a sacrifice instead. Just a few verses later, in the next chapter, we learn that Isaac's mother, Sarah, became ill and died. There are no references to whether she was ever aware of the attempted sacrifice of her son. We do know, however, that Isaac was Sarah's miracle. The promise from God that Abraham's wife would bear a child at ninety years old seemed unimaginable for him. Even Sarah had to laugh when she overheard that she would give birth!

Sarah may have initially questioned her ability to be a mother, but I bet she could not have imagined the role God had planned for Abraham as a father. Even more unbelievable than the fact that she would be having a child at her age would have been the realization that her miracle son would be offered as a sacrifice.

One of the daunting challenges of parenting is the inability to govern the role of your co-parent. As women begin to imagine and define motherhood, we also begin to form a paradigm in our minds of fatherhood. The varying circumstances in which a child is brought into this world create curiosity about how the co-parenting relationship will be established. *What type of father will he be? Will he work more or less? Is fighting over who gets up with the baby par for the course? Will we need to arrange a visitation schedule? How will he handle it when our daughter begins to date? Will our son be taught that men don't cry?*

Will he even be a part of the baby's life at all?

As a single parent, I had imagined all the things my children were missing by not having a constant male figure in their lives. I tried to fill in the gaps as much as I could, but I knew that it was impossible for me to play the role of both a mother and a father. After a failed marriage, I became even more concerned with the notion that my children were lacking fundamental principles only a father could provide. I found myself feeling guilt and shame when noticing other children walking into school with both parents by their side.

One of my primary goals as a single mother was for my children to feel and recognize that love is not confined to tradition. It was very important to me that my children recognize that family comes in all different shapes and sizes. My prayer was that we would not be so consumed with what we were lacking that we did not value what we had. Still, I imagine that on difficult days they were tempted, as was I, to imagine life with a man in the house. In the recesses of my mind I entertained many thoughts on what dual parenting would look like. I fantasized about cooking dinner while my husband helped the children with their homework. On really difficult days as a single mother I imagined I would come home to my make-believe husband in full Mr. Mom regalia. I can't even say I truly believed it was possible, but I enjoyed dreaming of a husband who moonlighted as a mind reader.

Then I actually met a man so in tune with my spirit that it seemed my fantasy would become a reality. One of the chief criteria I had before even contemplating marriage was that any man would have to love my children like they were his own. When God orchestrated the introduction to and love story with my current husband, it felt too good to be true.

My prayer was that we would not be so consumed with what we were lacking that we did not value what we had.

As we began to seriously discuss the possibilities of marriage, I had an honest conversation with him about the daddy issues my children were facing. I knew that the absence of a male figure in their lives would affect them in some way. My prayers were devoted to God's giving me the wisdom and faith to help guide them through the daddy insecurities that may await them. Touré, now my husband, communicated the paternal love and obligation God had given him for my children. My heart leaped as I witnessed how seriously he took the role of fatherhood with his three biological children.

I'm not sure that I'd ever witnessed a father as involved with or connected to his children. Instantly, the idea of fatherhood that existed in my mind seemed more tangible than ever before. I thought that once we married, the movie playing in my head would translate to reality, but I quickly learned my movie would need some editing. There are things innately unique to my role as a mother and as many things only a father's perspective can provide.

I had to avoid directing him on how to love my children my way and instead allow them to create their own bond. I must admit, initially I was overly critical of their interaction. I'd been a single parent for so long that I didn't appreciate the beauty of having additional support. It was a tough pill for me to swallow, but I had to realize that my children didn't need a male version of me. They needed to understand the distinct communication patterns and expressions of love that come from having two unique parents.

I had to realize that my children didn't need a male version of me. They needed to understand the distinct communication patterns and expressions of love that come from having two unique parents.

In time I learned to appreciate that we were wired differently. It may take several days before the empty cupboard begins to wear on his conscience, but he is the first to sense when one of the children has withdrawn. While it took prodding and multiple-choice questions to get the children to open up to me, he could break their walls down with a simple look of knowing compassion. True enough, we each offered something different, and I could not measure his offering based on my expectations.

Long before God ordered Touré's steps into my life, I think I'd become a bitter single mother. I was upset because I felt abandoned in the world of parenting. I wasn't sure that there was help in my future, but I knew that obstacles were bound to meet me on the journey. I couldn't help my children with their daddy issues until I confronted my own. My truth was that I was disappointed I'd have to face raising my children alone.

It was becoming increasingly evident that I would be exclusively responsible for managing the paternal disappointments my children were carrying in their hearts. The thought of their fathers avoiding the curveballs that come with parenting enraged me. I wasn't sure that I would be enough to spare them, and I was right. One day it dawned on me that parenting would require more than what I or the notion of an exceptional stepfather could offer. It would require our omnipresent God.

When Abraham and Isaac were traveling to the place in Moriah where the altar would be built for the burnt offering, Isaac stopped and asked Abraham why they weren't traveling with the sacrificial lamb. Abraham reassured him that God would provide the lamb once they reached their destination. Isaac could not have known the directions Abraham had received from God. It is safe to assume, had he known, that he would have had many more questions for his father. Unfortunately, he would not have been the only child who has had to question the value his life has to his parent.

This curiosity is not just isolated to the role of fatherhood, either.

Many of the people who have come into my life have dealt with the painful reality of not feeling wanted or accepted by one or both of their parents. Though the plight of fatherless children is far more sensationalized, there are many adults with adolescent wounds from parents who sacrificed their lives for far less righteous reasons than Abraham had. The tragic truths of drug addiction, incarceration, abuse, demanding careers, and countless other issues have robbed many of the family life they hoped to have. I've witnessed the stories of many who still feel bound to the altar they were left on. No story has been as painful to observe as the narrative of my own children.

The progression from enthusiastic expectation to constant rejection happened so rapidly I had no words formed to ease their frustration. They wanted to know why there wasn't a lamb that could be sacrificed instead of them. My young children were filled with questions about what could possibly be more important than their birthdays or first days of school. They needed to know why they were expendable. I could offer them no explanation that gave them consolation. They were too young to understand that God may have been using the distance as protection until their fathers were able to influence their lives positively and consistently. I resigned to listening to their words dipped in sorrow and wept on the inside. Becoming a parent either grows you up or makes you act like a child yourself. So many find themselves shrinking when faced with the magnitude of caring for another person more than they care for themselves.

That task becomes even more overwhelming when they've never experienced the type of care they feel they deserved.

There are many adults with adolescent wounds from parents who sacrificed their lives for far less righteous reasons than Abraham had.

The cycle of broken people breaking the hearts of those surrounding them often regenerates through many generations. Hurt people don't always intentionally hurt other people. It's just difficult to break free from the only emotions they've ever known. When pain becomes the norm, healing becomes the fear. Though I can't be sure, I believe the longer a parent is away, the easier it becomes to stay away. The days turn to months, months to years, and eventually they've been gone so long they aren't even sure how to come back. The realization that there will be questions that need answering and foundations that must be built tricks absentee parents into believing their children are better off without them. The aching for that missing parent never fully dissipates. It becomes tolerable at best, but having no knowledge of the other half that completes you leaves a scar.

> *The cycle of broken people breaking the hearts of those surrounding them often regenerates through many generations.*

I've been praying that the size of the scar on my children's lives will be as minimal as possible. My heart has been hoping that God will help my children to see that they have been fully equipped to overcome in spite of what they believe they're lacking.

The first week of school my daughter looked from the car window and saw a young boy with his mom and dad walking into the building. I'll never forget the sharp pain I felt when I heard her say, "I wish my dad could walk me to school." I know that life constantly reminds her of his absence. Commercials on television, storylines in books, and families coming into church repeatedly remind her of what she doesn't have.

My son has found his own way of coping. Once very expressive about his disappointment, he has begun to accept that no one, not even him, can force his dad to be present. As a mother, I'm not sure which posture was more painful to watch. On one hand, I knew his anticipation may not come to fruition, but at least he still had hope. Watching as hope drained and began to sound a bit like disdain was no walk in the park either.

Unfortunately, feelings of abandonment leave many children bound to altars when there were plenty of rams hidden in nearby bushes. How do we learn to teach our children to look beyond their perceived lack and trust that God has a plan?

I thought that my role as their mother was to advocate for their right to have a father. Challenging their dads to fulfill the roles their children and I desired became my mission. I employed every method I thought would incentivize change. From chastisement to encouragement, I hoped my pleas would convince them to take advantage of the remaining time they had to be active in our children's lives. Their inability to meet my demands with action left me with the realization that my children's fathers could only be motivated to change at their own pace and with God's grace. I'd begun to focus so heavily on what they were not doing that I wasn't giving nearly enough attention to areas I could improve. Their failure to meet expectations did not give me a license to avoid setting and exceeding new ones of my own.

I know in your time, Mary, family came in many compositions. Did you ever think the time would come when having concubines would be grounds for prosecution? I've read stories in the Bible of women like Hagar, the Egyptian slave who gave Abraham his first son but who was sent away because Sarah didn't want competition for Isaac. Or the story of Jochebed, the Hebrew mother who set her baby Moses in a floating basket on the Nile river to avoid the mass slaughtering of Hebrew boys. They both, and many others, had to amend their definitions of family to fit the conditions in which they lived.

My childhood did not force me to make those adjustments. My parents have been married my entire life. Though my father had to work quite a bit to provide the best possible life for us, I never had to wonder if I'd see him again. He may not have been present at every birthday party, but I never had to fight alone. As a teenager I lamented more than I care to admit that he and I didn't go for walks in the parks or share ice cream on warm days. Then I stopped focusing so much on what I missed and began to recognize the many things he made possible for my siblings and me.

God has made a provision for every void we've experienced and all harm we've survived.

Without his commitment and dedication, we never would have been exposed to a different side of life. The relentless force of his work ethic unleashed the boundaries of our dreams. Quite frankly, if it weren't for him, you wouldn't be reading this book.

It wasn't until I became personally familiar with the demands of single parenting that I realized we all have our own set of issues. Your dad can be in your life each day and you can still find an area where he could have improved. Your mother may have made the best cookies in town, but never mastered communicating effectively.

The more room we make for compassionate understanding, the less space we have for unforgiveness, doubt, and fear.

I guess what I'm trying to say is that there are no perfect parents or families. We all come with dilemmas and struggles that require faith to overcome. All that we can strive to offer is our absolute best. We don't even get to assess whether our co-parent's best was good enough. Our freedom lies in our refusal to be bound by what we think we've missed. God has made a provision for every void we've experienced and all harm we've survived. As a mother, I pray to never let my fears interfere with the faith I have in God's perfect plan for my children. I hope to never lose the conviction to become better even when the opportunity to become bitter is alluring.

Moments before the angel Gabriel paid you a visit, you were planning a life with Joseph. When you learned the father of your firstborn wouldn't be the one you expected him to be, were you ever disappointed? We see in Luke 1:46 how your heart rejoiced in the new path your feet would voyage. Though the road ahead was uncertain, you trusted the One who ordered your steps.

Your life has taught me the requirement of humility in parenting. The more room we make for compassionate understanding, the less space we have for unforgiveness, doubt, and fear. I may not be able to give my children the father they've imagined or the traditional upbringing they see in this world, but I can show them the power in trusting our heavenly Father with every issue of our hearts.

4

my child is different

Everyone who heard him was amazed at his understanding and his answers.

Luke 2:47

*D*ear Mary,

As if the moment Gabriel visited you wasn't enough, when the wise men sought you out after Christ's birth, it must have been very obvious that raising Him would be different. Still, it appears you tried to create an environment that would allow His gift time to fully develop. I can only imagine the alarming fear you must have felt when you couldn't locate Him on the journey from Jerusalem to Nazareth after the Passover feast. I can't help but ask, was it difficult to create a typical upbringing for your Son who was obviously so special? Sure, everyone is unique in his or her own way, but there's something to be said when that difference cannot be hidden. As much as you tried to give Him an ordinary existence, He could not be confined to the notion of normal. It took four or five days to travel from Jerusalem to Nazareth on foot. Somewhere amid all of your friends and family traveling together, you thought that Jesus was with you. Luke teaches us that it wasn't until you began searching for Him that you realized He wasn't there with all the others.

Most parents desire for their children to avoid the pressure of fitting in, but sometimes when the difference comes on display, we wish they could blend in. In the comfort of our homes, the nuances that make our children who they are can be tolerated with love, understanding, and compassion.

How can we protect them from a world that may not be so accepting of their individuality? That commission becomes even more delicate when what makes them exceptional has negative social implications.

In 2010, Kate Davis and her husband, David Heilbroner, produced and directed a documentary that allows a personal glimpse into families struggling with the abnormal behavior of their children. *Diagnosis Bipolar: Five Families Searching for Answers* instantly captured my attention when I flipped to it on television. When interviewed about what compelled Davis to tell the story of these families, she shared:

> Having children myself, I have witnessed extreme mood swings and wondered at times where my own kids fall on the spectrum of "normalcy." Then I began seeing articles on pediatric bipolar disorder in which parents were criticized for medicating their children, where the diagnosis was clearly the center of intense debate, and I wondered what life was like from the families' perspectives. It seemed to me that their experiences were being overlooked, often misunderstood, and needed to be portrayed.[1]

I completely understand her logic. I imagine every parent at some point begins to witness conduct from their children that makes them wonder if they're experiencing routine adolescent development or if an imbalance that is out of their control is occurring. From the moment our children begin visiting doctors, we're asked a series of questions to gauge the progress of their mental and physical growth. We know that babies begin rolling over as early as four months. Around twelve months a baby should be able to say a couple of first words. The pressure to meet these milestones continues well into adulthood, actually. In grade school a child's ability to learn and comprehend is measured by tests and assignments. Failure to meet these standards creates insecurities in both parents and children.

Our insecurities are only heightened when we begin to compare our children to friends and relatives who aren't just meeting the bar, but getting there early. I'll never forget dropping my son off at his childcare facility and hearing another mother recount how she had managed to potty train her eighteen-month-old son! I had been spending weekend after weekend, using method after method, to try to teach my almost-three-year-old how to use the potty. I suppose the convenience of my wiping his bottom was just too sweet of a deal to pass up, because he was downright refusing to learn.

After hearing the other mom singing the praises of her son, I began to wonder if I needed

Our insecurities are only heightened when we begin to compare our children to friends and relatives who aren't just meeting the bar, but getting there early.

the intervention of a professional. So I did what any frantic person in my position would do. I called my mother! She immediately eased my concerns by reminding me that every child is different. She insisted that I not jump to conclusions. A few grueling months after that conversation, my son got out of the bed one morning, walked into the bathroom, lifted the toilet lid, and did his business. I never had to change him again. It seemed like all of a sudden things just clicked for him. My concerns and remaining diapers disappeared just as quickly.

Things were a bit more complicated for the parents of Liv, one of the children featured in Davis's documentary. At the age of four, Liv was diagnosed as bipolar and had been hospitalized twice for extended periods of time. Bipolar disorder, formerly called manic depression, is a mental illness that brings severe high and low moods and changes in sleep patterns, energy, thinking, and behavior.[2] In *Diagnosis Bipolar*, Liv's mother recounts a time when her daughter was placed in a facility for care. It took seven adults to restrain her daughter. Yet in the very next scene we see an innocent Liv riding in the car with her father, anticipating the day when she'll be the legal age to drive. Her conversation is not unlike discussions other children her age are having, but it does exemplify the stark contrast of her reality.

Another time, a shopping trip turns into a wrestling match in the parking lot when Liv doesn't get a timely snack—and becomes incredibly angry. We watch as her mother struggles to convince her to return to the car. Instead, she sits in the middle of the street, yelling and kicking. Her mother's face begins to flush a bright red as she tries to lift Liv from the ground. Referring to her self-conscious struggle to help her daughter, she relates how tough it becomes when people gawk and just assume that she's a mom who doesn't know how to control her daughter. But she also indicates that eventually, she had to quit caring what other people might think.

As much as we'd like to protect our children from the world that may misjudge them, there are moments when we can no longer conceal what makes them rare. Finding Jesus in the temple courts surrounded by teachers and priests must have been one of those moments for you, Mary. As relieved as you were to find Him, did you wonder how much of who

He is had been revealed? You must have arrived just in time, because it wasn't until much later that Christ's ministry began. If the teachers had realized in that moment who He was, there probably would have been a demand for him to start His ministry right then and there. Somehow you managed to shield Him so expertly that little is known about the eighteen years between the temple and the baptism that initiated His journey to the cross.

Though you knew from the moment of conception that He was different, you did not force what made Him unique to become His label. Had you broadcast the story of Christ's formation in your womb to everyone you encountered, surely you would have been met with skepticism and disapproval. The fulfillment of His purpose rested in your ability to teach Him how to guard His heart for the mandate God had on His life. You did not rely on the sole power of your words to administer this lesson. Instead, you allowed your actions, discretion, and wisdom to show Him. You led by example even when you didn't understand Jesus fully. In Luke 2, after you've finally tracked down your Son and confronted Him about His whereabouts, His reply may have confused you, but it did not dissuade you from being his mother.

> "Why were you searching for me?" he asked. "Didn't you know I had to be in my Father's house?"
>
> Luke 2:49–51

The event that took place in the temple is the first recognized record of Jesus speaking. Even though His words left you confused, you did not toss them away as jargon. Instead you stored both the words and His obedience in your heart as gems. I thought I was the only one who found herself confused by the actions or words of her children. I once used those moments to formulate possible answers or consequences for their actions. Your heart response challenged me to recognize that some of life's most confusing questions often require us to have the faith to keep moving forward. Twice in Luke 2 it is written that you treasured in your heart every indication of Christ's distinction. Maybe our prayer shouldn't be to change our children into people we can understand, but rather to have the patience to be still while we learn who they are.

As difficult as Liv's mother's struggle in the documentary is, it also becomes increasingly inspiring. Without the help of a formal medical education, she has learned the many intricate layers of the human psyche. Life has no barriers for a mother determined to save her child, as we see in an intimate glimpse into Liv's nighttime ritual with her mom. Exhausted from a long day of mental and emotional ups and down, she's tucked into bed, but not before hearing her mother sweetly whisper, "Good night, princess." Within one day this mother has experienced a plethora of different emotions, but treasured in her heart is the truth of who her daughter is: a princess. Maybe she doesn't quite understand the things her daughter has done or said that day, but she accepts her and fights for her all along the way.

There is no way of guesstimating what discoveries we will unearth as we raise our children. I am a young mom, and even I have learned that there will be moments when I'm not exactly sure who they have become. As they grow and are exposed, more of who they are will be revealed. I believe we have a responsibility to avoid labeling lives God is still developing. Perhaps that's why we must learn to treasure in our hearts the clues we receive along the way. If it were possible to keep our children nestled safely away from opposition that wouldn't be gentle with their vulnerability, we'd all sign up for that. A sobering reality is the unlikelihood of that desire ever being realized. Our assignment then becomes teaching them to navigate the world without despising their differences.

Being ashamed of who we are taints who we will become. When we rid ourselves of the many labels we receive from society, we explore the beauty of our authenticity. I truly believe that God lives inside of each of us. We cannot forget that each breath is a miracle. Our conditions may be different, but God's grace is capable of using every affliction for His glory.

When we feel full of despair, it isn't always evident how our struggle could ever help others. But it is not our duty to understand how God will utilize the distinction of our lives to help other people. All that we can do is strive not to reject the very characteristic God can use to manifest His perfect will for our lives. We must recognize that we have been divinely appointed to raise the children God has given us. No level of judgment, anxiety, or frustration should rob us of the knowledge that we are equipped to handle the challenge of rearing children society may not know how to accept. If we instill that validation cannot come from man, but only through trust in God's perfect plan, they will have peace no man can steal. It's

We have a responsibility to avoid labeling lives God is still developing.

much easier to write that charge than to activate it, but then I remember my child's life depends on it. If I don't believe it, then I can't teach them to believe it either.

I pray that mothers across the world can suspend their disbelief long enough to find a mustard seed of faith. We can choose to no longer care what others think long enough to embrace our courage and withstand the humiliation that humility carries. I must admit, had I witnessed in person the struggle between Liv and her mother, I would have given her a judgmental stare. With no knowledge of her struggle or insight to her dilemma, I would have become the very person she was hoping to shield her daughter from. I am a more compassionate person because they shared their life with us.

I don't know where those five families are on their journey of searching for treatment. I wish I knew that the road got easier for them. Nevertheless, I do know that their lives challenged me to build a reservoir of unconditional love for my children and to never stop safeguarding the gifts inside of them.

5

i didn't make dinner

And he said: "Truly I tell you, unless you change and become like little children, you will never enter the kingdom of heaven. Therefore, whoever takes the lowly position of this child is the greatest in the kingdom of heaven. And whoever welcomes one such child in my name welcomes me."

Matthew 18:3–5

*D*ear Mary,

It is well after His ascension, and the impression your Son's life made on the world continues to touch people all over the world. In the three years of His ministry, he traveled all over sharing powerful parables, performing undeniable miracles, and bringing reformation to a people in danger of becoming stagnant. The sacrifice of His life impacted the world so greatly that those who believed began to identify themselves as Christians. The symbol of the cross has infiltrated nearly every part of the world. In December 2011, the Pew Research Center reported that there were 2.18 billion Christians in the world.[1] That is more than seven times the population of the world in the days of Christ! I have spent the bulk of my life in church hearing of His works. I have seen countless souls set free by accepting Jesus as their personal Savior. As silly as it may sound, though, I never fully trusted that His power could break the chains on *my* life.

John 3:16 states that God sacrificed His only Son so that those who believed in Him would not perish, but have everlasting life. It wasn't until I was faced with my own devastation that I realized how easy it is to be alive but not truly living. Many of the challenges we face convince us to no longer live life to its fullest. Instead we settle for the security of the known and never explore the truth of who we can become through Christ. It's difficult to accept His unadulterated love when you're still battling with imperfections. I knew how to speak as Christians did, but when the time came for me to place those words into action, I was too afraid of failing to trust the power I spoke of.

It wasn't until I was faced with my own devastation that I realized how easy it is to be alive but not truly living.

I know that quite a bit of my struggle was rooted in the perception that people would pass judgment on my starting place. I came from a family of believers, but I still had to know God for myself.

More than a decade before I was born, my father had found the purpose for his existence. His keen understanding of the Word and heart-wrenching delivery have led some of the most wayward souls to the truth of salvation. He met my mother while operating in his God-given gift. I'm sure he'd be the first to tell you, if it weren't for her, he could not have found the strength to continue and subsequently could not have shared his divine gift with millions. Together, he and my mother led a group of believers from Charleston, West Virginia, to Dallas, Texas, spreading the good news of Jesus Christ. I don't think they could have known that their willingness to share this news would change the lives of so many, but it has.

I'm also positive that they didn't realize the level of scrutiny and attack that comes with serving that many people. I can't say they wouldn't have done it, but I do believe they would have taken extra precautions before moving forward.

Mary, you must have felt the same way after it became clear that you were with child. You came from a good Hebrew family and had found a good man in your fiancé, Joseph. And then the angel showed up with a message that clearly terrified you at first. Talk about not knowing what to expect when you're expecting! But you surrendered your ego and let go of the approval of others, trusting God with the most intimate parts of you—your body, your heart, your soul.

I wrote in my memoir, *Lost and Found*, that being surrounded by so many people made me feel more insecure than empowered. It seemed like the Christian walk had only two paths: miraculous recovery or recurrent delivery. Those who fell into the category of miraculous recovery seemed to no longer struggle and instantly began getting everything right. That illusion being true or false made no difference, because it was all assessed from my limited observation and their opaque transparency. After taking inventory of the many issues existing in my heart, I knew that I couldn't make them disappear that quickly.

You surrendered your ego and let go of the approval of others, trusting God with the most intimate parts of you—your body, your heart, your soul.

Then there were those that I saw coming to the altar each Sunday. In my mind, they lived with little to no conviction six days throughout the week, then came to accept their clean slate for the next week. It appeared that they were taking advantage of the grace they'd been given.

I knew that my life was a work in progress. I convinced myself it was better to figure things out on my own than to pretend I was someone I truly wasn't.

As unfortunate as my resignation may sound, I believe that I benefited from it in the long run. My walk with Christ is neither forced nor fictitious. I personally came to learn the power of the blood shed on Calvary when I ran out of places to run. The insecurity of not fitting in had created a void in my heart that I wanted the love of a person to fill. I tried to dive into the depths of another person's soul so that I could forget the aching of my own. The deeper I fell into them, the less time I had to worry about me. Each of those attempts backfired until I realized I was searching for a Savior that I never lost. I spent more time than I care to admit reminding myself that my past disqualified me from receiving the redemptive power of Christ. I never realized that there was no qualification process; He was giving it to me freely. Not because of who I am or what I had done, but because of who He is. Accepting and exploring the depths of Christ's gift has been my most fascinating adventure. It has required that I release my pride and inhibitions and allow every area of my life to be accessible for divine transformation.

It took me some time, but I have come a looonng way. I knew that my children would follow my example, so I had to decide what I desired my life to communicate. Did I want them to become servants of people, or to withhold nothing so that God could get the glory out of their lives? So when I made the decision to divorce, it wasn't one that I made lightly. In many respects, divorce is just as taboo now as it was in your time. But I knew that my marriage wasn't built to glorify God, but rather to serve two broken people. I'd married in an effort to find a savior, not a partner.

While the plans that God has for our lives are all unique and different, I knew that I could not fully give my heart to

Him until I took it back from the pseudo-saviors I had deified along the way. I learned to no longer hold them to the impossible standard of perfection. The failure to meet those unrealistic expectations left me more fragile than I had been before. I knew I wasn't being fair to them or to myself. With the exception of your Son, we're all flawed humans, and until I learned to accept agape love, I could never give it.

In my darkest days my children taught me the necessity of unconditional love in a life full of conditions. There isn't one thing that I would not do for their well-being. I craved to offer them the most genuine version of who I am. I knew that desire would require me to have an authentic encounter with the perfect One. My children are yet young and have not fully discovered the depths of who I have become, but I wanted to live a life that I would be proud to answer to them about. I will not be able to say that I made all of the right choices, but I desire to say that I strived to take each step with God.

My children taught me the necessity of unconditional love in a life full of conditions.

To be honest, I did not have much time to be ashamed of my divorcée label, because I needed to focus on being a full-time single mother. Providing, nurturing, disciplining, and educating my two children required my undivided attention. Making sure they had a roof over their heads, stayed on target in school, and ate well-balanced meals became my priority. As much as I wanted to offer them a gourmet menu each evening, there was simply not enough time in the day.

This world has certainly made a few terrifying turns for the worse, but there are more than a few advancements that have made the job of a parent easier. One of those inventions is food that can be prepared literally within minutes. We're not talking manna here, either! There are numerous options to cater to the demands of hectic schedules. They aren't always the most nutritious meals, but the convenience has assisted me on days when neither time nor finances would allow for something more elaborate. I must admit that I have often felt guilty for indulging too frequently in the quick access I have to these alternatives.

One evening when I could not bear to go out but did not have time to prepare a full meal before bedtime, I made my own form of fast food. A quick assessment of the items in my kitchen left me with limited options for dinner. I wanted to provide at least one vegetable, one form of protein, a fruit, and grains. While I did not have the ideal items in the kitchen to receive a nod from the USDA, I decided to make do. It took me less than ten minutes to whip up their meal. I found some frozen chicken that could be cooked in the microwave, sprinkled olive oil over kale to make chips in the oven, and found a cup of yogurt just days from expiring. I placed the meal on our good plates and yelled, "Dinner is served!"

This may not seem like too shabby of a meal in your opinion, but I declare I could feel the judgment from neighborhood moms who had slaved in their kitchens that day. It did not take long for it to dawn on me that I could not allow myself to be in imaginary competition. I had to give myself permission to grow into my expectations. It may not have been the meal I wish I could have given them, but it is a meal that another child was not fortunate enough to have.

Later that evening as Makenzie was preparing for bed, she made it a point to ask me if we could have the same dinner tomorrow. It dawned on me that I'd spent so long beating myself up for a meal that I didn't feel was up to par that I never realized just how much my daughter had enjoyed it. The kale chips had even shown me a new way to get her to eat her vegetables.

I was challenged to remember when the disciples asked your Son, "Who is the greatest in the kingdom of heaven?" His answer was that we must all become as children if we desire to enter heaven. My daughter had no awareness of the finer meals she could have been consuming. She was still basking in the fact that dinner was finished early enough that we had time to indulge in an epic coloring competition. All she knew was that her tummy was full and her heart was happy. I wondered when I had become my biggest critic. I'd reduced my role as a mother down to my ability to effectively follow a diagram every evening. Meanwhile, I had ignored the radiating smile emitting from her face.

I could not allow myself to be in imaginary competition. I had to give myself permission to grow into my expectations.

I needed to make sure that I didn't become so consumed with thinking like an adult that I failed to truly love as a child. As much as we hope to instill in our children, we have only a few precious years to learn from their innocence. My new goal as a mother is to listen as much as I speak. Mary, I appreciate the way you listened to all the angel told you before you responded and accepted the gift he told you God wanted to give you. Later, when Jesus was growing up and visiting the temple, He clearly had something to say. I suspect that you listened to His teaching even when He was a boy and realized you had so much to learn from Him.

This has afforded me the opportunity to be reminded of the unparalleled hope I once possessed. Long before I was introduced to reasons to be insecure and before my ambition could be contaminated by doubt, I believed all things were possible for me. I could become a doctor, lawyer, actress, and dancer all because it was in my heart to do so. When I was a child, forgiveness came easy and scars faded quickly. Christ must have taught you more lessons than you even realized, Mary. I have learned from your relationship the value in being your child's student.

6

letting grow

"Who is my mother, and who are my brothers?" Pointing to his disciples, he said, "Here are my mother and my brothers. For whoever does the will of my Father in heaven is my brother and sister and mother."

Matthew 12:48–50

*D*ear Mary,

I'm not sure what makes parenting scarier: the fact that a child's protection and development depends solely on you, or that one day it won't depend on you at all. Many of us mothers gladly build our entire lives around our children. Everything down to what time we eat and when we can go to the restroom depends on where our children are in their day. As they grow older and their needs change, our lives find a rhythm, but our mind remains fixed on them. We spend just as much energy invested in their social progression, academic courses, and extracurricular activities as they do, perhaps even more. While we strive to meet all their present needs, our ultimate goal is that they no longer need to be sustained by us at all. If our hopes, prayers, faith, and action come into alignment, the babies we start off holding will eventually become responsible enough to live their lives without our constant support.

Though my children are still years from adulthood, I am constantly bombarded with the pressure to raise self-sufficient adults. The desire to instill integrity, responsibility, and sound moral character hardly ever escapes me. It haunts every piece of advice and discipline I dole out to them. I often wonder how you guided Jesus' foray into adulthood knowing that He would face seemingly insurmountable odds. It appears as if those odds did not dissuade you from infusing tenacity and courage into Jesus' life. Is it possible for our children to become too brave?

In Matthew 12 we find Jesus in one of the most significant times of His ministry. He was surrounded by His disciples and a great multitude, sharing wisdom and insight about His mission on earth. By this point in the text, He was no longer the twelve-year-old boy within His mother's reach. Instead, He was a confident man shining a light into darkness and bringing revelation to tradition. I can only imagine how you looked on with pride as you realized that, in spite of the twists and turns your life had taken, Jesus had found His way right to where He belonged. In a moment of anxiety, a mother can't help but wonder how her children will be affected by the culture and environment in which they've been formed.

You spent much of Jesus' early years hoping to maintain the mystery of His divinity. While there were a few close calls, you were able to shelter His development so that when the time was right, He could walk into his position with authority. And boy, did He!

Thousands upon thousands surrounded Him as He spoke truth. It must have taken a few moments for news of your arrival to travel to Him from where you stood with His brothers (see Matthew 12:46–50). I believe that a part of me would've hoped that news of my presence would give my son an extra sense of covering or protection, but I never could have been prepared to hear the words that came from Christ's mouth. As He rebuked the notion of familial relationships taking precedence over spiritual connections, was your heart forever bruised? His brothers stood there with you, watching as their older brother disowned the idea of exclusivity to a family yet embraced the multitudes that were willing to believe in Him.

How do you handle no longer having a coveted place in your child's life? How can we maintain confidence that though our children are transforming in front of our eyes, it's not because they no longer need us, but rather because they need the experiences that lead to their destiny more?

One summer morning I looked my son in his face and could've sworn that I saw the face of a man. I rubbed my eyes, focused more closely, and saw the face of my baby boy return. I thought it was just a happenstance, but the same thing happened a few more times over the summer. His face was losing the plump cheeks where I once landed my kisses. The words from his mouth were no longer airy and light, but rather grounded with bass and careful wisdom.

I traveled more this year for work than I ever have. I made sure the trips were spaced apart so that I could remain present in my children's lives. I still couldn't help but feel like things had changed overnight. It was nearly heartbreaking for me when I noticed my son's language transition from calling me Mommy to calling me Mom. It may sound silly, but there's something sweet and innocent about the extra syllable on the end. I suppose that's a part of life, but I was having a difficult time adapting. I knew that I wasn't the fourteen-year-old girl who had given birth to him anymore, but for some reason I thought he'd stay the same little boy I'd been toting on my hip. Even when he grew too big for me to hold, we hugged so often that I never lost the feeling of having him in my arms.

Mothers with older sons warned me the time would come when my son would no longer be infatuated with my presence. I would nod my head and pretend like I was prepared for that day to come, yet on the inside I shrugged their advice away. I was certain that wouldn't happen to me. Our bond was different because we'd grown up together. From the day he was born, we were stuck together like glue. It was only after several years in grade school that he realized how much younger I was than his friends' mothers. Up until then, Malachi had no clue how unusual our situation was. All he knew was that I was his mother. I opened communication so that he could express how it made him feel. "I think it's cool I have a young mom," he said. I had to thank God he felt that way. I know that isn't always the outcome for the children of teen parents.

Interestingly enough, our age difference did not protect me from the theories most children have about their parents. He wasn't too trusting of my fashion sense, music taste, or selection in films. It wasn't until the summer of 2014 that I started to believe there may be some veracity to his claims. One day, I could faintly hear the hum of a familiar tune as he came down the stairs. I grabbed the nearest hairbrush and began to sing along. I was almost to the chorus when I realized that my instrumentalist was staring silently (and dare I say horrifyingly) at me. I froze my performance to investigate his silence.

"That's not what I was humming."

Unable to accept his rejection, I re-hummed the song I was almost sure I'd heard him performing. He shook his head and climbed back up the stairs as if it had never happened. My bottom lip slowly began to poke out as I recalled a time when my solo would've turned into our duet. My baby was turning into a young man. There wasn't much I could do to slow the pace of time, so I made extra effort to learn his interests. I became very curious to acquaint myself with who he was becoming.

As I began to observe his transformation, I noticed the roots of the seeds placed inside of him beginning to cultivate. His sense of humor was witty, sarcastic, and intelligent. I could no longer speak over his head and became fearful that sometimes he was speaking over mine. Not to mention he would soon literally tower over me. I didn't have to tilt my head down the least bit to make eye contact. Nearly eye-to-eye and nose-to-nose, he was only an inch from reaching my height. This little human that I brought into the world would inevitably be taller than me. I tried to make him promise he wouldn't grow any more, but we knew that was a vow he was bound to break.

I find myself searching his face for signs of the baby I once held, yet hoping to catch a sneak peek into the masculine features that were beginning their formation. A dark tint had even begun forming on his upper lip, making way for the debut of his teenage mustache. I wasn't sure how my role as a mother should transform with him, but I was hoping I'd stop reminiscing long enough to remain relevant in his world.

It all felt so foreign to me, but I knew that at the same time he was evolving, I was too. Did you ever get so mesmerized by Christ's transformation that you stopped changing yourself? I was struggling with saying good-bye to the childhood quirks that had been exchanged for adolescent mood swings.

Meanwhile, my personal evolution had less to do with my hormones and more to do with creating long-term stability. After an incredible high in my career, I was faced with the reality that I would have to relocate if I wanted to continue to grow. Traveling back and forth for meetings was beginning to wear on my finances and relationship with my kids.

After sharing my reality with my confidants, they all agreed I had come to a fork in the road. I could choose not to maximize my potential and stay in the safety of my comfort zone, or I could walk on water. I've always been a planner, so I began to prayerfully consider all of the logistics relocating would necessitate. I hesitated to make a decision until I was sure the presence of God was ordering my direction. The moment I was sure of my decision, I made a phone call to my parents. I went over the more minute details with my mother. Creating a timeline for moving, determining whether to rent or sell my home, and researching schools in the area I was moving to were all settled before the phone conversation ended.

There would still be several weeks before the plan was activated, but having the blessing and support of my parents gave me the thrust I needed to push forward. It was only a couple of weeks after our conversation that my mother texted me, "I didn't realize you were moving." I'm not sure if I'm the only daughter whose mother has selective memory, but this wasn't a rare occurrence.

Depending on what else is going on in the world, whether celebrity news or a plethora of business decisions, my mother can completely forget a conversation. I reminded her of the detailed discussion we had just weeks prior. "I know. I just didn't realize it was coming so soon," she replied. Though the situations were completely different, I identified with the emotion hidden in between the words. She didn't realize how quickly I was growing up. Instantly roles were reversed, and I was now the child reminding my mother that the soundtrack of my life was changing. We were both dealing with the harrowing fact that no matter how tightly we held on to our babies, we needed to let them grow.

In Matthew 12, strangers had traveled from all over that day you waited to speak with your Son. If you're anything like my mother, you smiled brightly as you watched Him fulfill the purpose of His presence on earth. Did you ever feel like you didn't fit in His life anymore? I'm sure you patiently watched as tears undoubtedly formed in the eyes of those who heard His message.

It can be bittersweet to celebrate your children's freedom when their lives have been sustained because of their connections to you.

By the fifth week of gestation, the umbilical cord is developed between a mother and her unborn fetus. The cord is formed to supply nutrients, oxygen, and blood to the baby. At birth that cord is severed, but the importance of its role cannot be diminished. Though it is cut mere moments after labor has ended, researchers have discovered stem cells in the cord blood that can treat diseases, prompting parents to opt to store the cord blood from their pregnancies as a precaution to treat a potential future illness. The facilities that provide storage for families who choose this option are called cord blood banks.

It can be bittersweet to celebrate your child's freedom when his life has been sustained because of his tie to you.

There is a peace of mind that comes with knowing this option exists in the unfortunate event a child becomes ill. The cord that once sustained a fetus in the womb has the ability to save the child's life even when he is well beyond the connection to his mother's womb.

The shift in relationship dynamic between my mother and me has taught me an invaluable example that I model with my children. Regardless of how quickly time passes by or culture changes the content of our conversations, we will forever be connected. "How can I be so happy for you but sad for me?" my mother asked as she said her good-byes to her grandchildren. Life may separate us from connections as we know them, but our hearts become banks that accumulate the wisdom, joy, and love of those moments.

> *Life may separate us from connections as we know them, but our hearts become banks that accumulate the wisdom, joy, and love of those moments.*

The wealth our hearts receive from the accumulation of all those God things becomes a part of who we are. As much as I will miss my mother, I look forward to the many times when I stop mid-action as I realize I'm doing something just as she would have done it. I'm amazed at how her exact words unintentionally come out of my mouth. Our relationship cannot be constrained to geographical location. Because I was a part of her, she will always be a part of me. Life is guaranteed to change, and that will demand growth, but the cords of love that bind a family can never be broken.

I know history proves this to be true, because there are moments when I look in her eyes and see her mother staring back at me. More than once I've found myself tormented with grandmother envy. I was nine years old when my grandmother earned her wings and heaven called her name. I guard the memories I do have of her close to my chest. The smell of cherry almond–scented lotion never wafts past my nose without my remembering her putting lotion on us in a hotel room at one of the conferences my father's ministry hosted. She was a stickler for staying moisturized. My older brother does an impression of her that nearly puts us all in stitches from laughing so hysterically. "Put some lotion on those ashy elbows!" he yells when giving his best Virginia Lee Jamison imitation. I remember how much care she took in making sure we were presented neatly and appropriately every opportunity she was given.

It's been almost twenty years since she passed away, but her spirit lives on in the most beautiful, petite, and graceful being: my mother. My house is brimming with clothes, socks, jackets, and sweaters randomly purchased for my children throughout the year by their doting grandmother. Not much compares to the look on their faces when they recount the stories of being with their granny. It's been said that grandparents are more lenient with their grandchildren than they were with their children. My father proves there is some legitimacy to this train of thinking—he turns into a teddy bear at the sound of their voices. But I can't apply that rule to my mother. I can't even feign jealousy at their obsession with her, either. She is the best mother I've ever known. With God's grace I'll become to them all that she's been to me.

> *We may have to tweak our roles to give room for our children to flourish, but we never fully release them. The task of motherhood and all it requires never completely vanishes.*

I don't know how you handled hearing your Son tell an audience full of people that they were all His brother, sister, and mother. If I were you, I think it would have stung for just a minute. When the sting wore off and I came to my senses, I hope I would have remembered that letting go and letting grow have two completely different meanings. For mothers, it can be difficult making a distinction between the two. We may have to tweak our roles to give room for our children to flourish, but we never fully release them. They can even grow to tower over us or to answer a purpose that links them to many others, but the task of motherhood and all it requires never completely vanishes.

I'm certain time will force me to remember the words I have written above. My young children will mature and experience milestones that change the essence of our connection. I can only hope that I'm never convinced that I am no longer needed. I pray that I will rest confidently in the fact that God is with us, and He'll show me how to mother them in their new season.

7

i'm a working mom

"Suppose one of you has a hundred sheep and loses one of them. Doesn't he leave the ninety-nine in the open country and go after the lost sheep until he finds it? And when he finds it, he joyfully puts it on his shoulders and goes home. Then he calls his friends and neighbors together and says, 'Rejoice with me; I have found my lost sheep.'"

Luke 15:4–6

*D*ear Mary,

     I was watching a movie with my daughter and son after a long but rewarding week of school and work. I allow them to pick our family activity on the weekends, but I must admit I do so with bated breath. My children's imaginations have the tendency to run a bit wild. Their idea of fun often requires more energy than I can offer. Luckily, this weekend was different. All they wanted was to pile in my bed and have a sleepover. I was ecstatic that I could change into comfortable clothes and doze in and out of sleep as we had our movie marathon.

     After making me promise that I would stay awake for one full movie, they began the agonizing process of selecting a movie. The process of choosing the film often becomes more emotionally investing than actually watching the film. My daughter enjoys movies with princesses, talking animals, and glitter. Her brother, on the contrary, likes movies with sarcastic humor, adventure, and thrilling plot lines. As they engaged in gripping debate, I chimed in periodically that the likelihood of my falling asleep was increasing rapidly.

     My father began using film as a means of outreach for people who would not venture into churches. Whenever we have these sleepovers, my daughter tries to watch a film that her Big Daddy has had a hand in producing. One of his recent projects, *Heaven Is For Real*, centers around a boy who goes to heaven and back after an emergency surgery. When the movie made its debut, my daughter was one of its biggest enthusiasts. She has a poster hanging in her room and a T-shirt she's worn so many times I've had to hide it. Needless to say, when she can't persuade her brother to indulge in movies featuring castles, catchy tunes, and choreography, she uses her Big Daddy trump card. Malachi can usually sense when the "support the family" speech is on the way and begins preparing his argument.

"Makenzie, we watched that last time," he began.

I just sat back and watched, recognizing that neither of them had any idea that they were more entertaining than any film that has yet to be produced.

"I just think it would make Big Daddy happy," Makenzie replied.

Tit for tat, they debated while listing the different options available on the television screen. I knew things were getting heated when the movie covers stopped scrolling across the screen—because my kids' attention was directed at one another.

Frustrated and running out of points, Makenzie yelled with righteous indignation, "IT'S A MOVIE ABOUT JESUS, CHI!" I think she was hoping that she could sway his decision by questioning his salvation. It didn't work. Amused but growing tired, I gave them thirty seconds to pick a movie or retreat to their bedrooms.

They landed on a classic film starring legendary talents—*The Wiz.*

Almost forty years after *The Wizard of Oz* made its cinematic debut, this more urban version of the film was released with an all-black cast and depicts the essence of the African

American experience. Though I hadn't yet been born when *The Wiz* was released, the film has left an indelible impression that reaches many generations. It's one of those movies I was raised hearing I *must* see. To be honest, I wasn't a huge fan of the original version, so I wasn't too inclined to watch the remake. There may have even been a few times growing up when I pretended that I'd watched it just to spare myself from embarrassment.

So when my son and daughter mutually agreed to watch it, I was excited. "Oh, I've never seen *The Wiz*," I mentioned as the movie began to start playing. My son instantly paused the movie, shocked by my confession. His exact words to me: "Mom, I'm more black than you are. I've seen *The Wiz!*" I didn't really know how to feel about the fact that he'd called me out. I was even more concerned that I think he may have been right. Since he challenged me, I was even more determined to stay awake for the entire movie.

Immediately, all of my attention was drawn to the character of Dorothy, played by legendary singer Diana Ross. The lyrics of the song and the character's all too familiar questioning of her identity intrigued me.

Once Dorothy is swept away by a blizzard into the strange fictitious Land of Oz, the first encounter she has is with creatures from the land. Instantly, they thank her profusely for a timely arrival that has rescued them from evil. Completely dumbfounded by their praises, Dorothy's sole reply is a plea for directions back home. In a quivering yet innocent voice, Dorothy begins to sing the fears she has of being in the strange new land.

I identified with the words immediately.

My biggest fear was that my children would lack the security and support they deserved. Yet how could I offer them something I was yet searching for myself? There's a parable in the Bible about a shepherd leaving his flock of one hundred sheep because one goes missing. If each sheep represents a responsibility, and all but one are safe, it seems completely plausible to search for the one that is lost. But what happens when it feels as though many of your sheep have scattered? Life has an uncanny ability to leave us grasping at straws when we least expect it. Much like the character in *The Wiz*, many women have found that life drops them and their children in the middle of the unexpected.

As if starting over in life isn't challenging enough, doing so with the eyes of little people watching you adds a new dimension of struggle. How can we save our children when we feel lost ourselves? I pray that life teaches me how to prioritize the many responsibilities of my life, but above all I hope I have the ability to admit when I need some extra covering from above. You must have had some very difficult decisions to make while raising Jesus. There must have been times in which you had to determine what to chase and what to allow to slip away. As you ran from city to city avoiding the attacks threatened on Christ's life, did you ever feel as though despair was chasing you even though faith guided you?

I discovered a gift worth treasuring buried under a mountain of insecurities.

It just so happened that the path of my life had led me into unknown territory, just like you, Mary. How scary it must have been to know that your baby's life was threatened by someone as powerful as King Herod. Then having to travel once again—this time with a newborn all the way to Egypt. You seemed to have handled life's curve balls with a grace grounded in God's grace. How else to explain the way you consistently endured the exploration of the unexpected?

My Egypt was much less life-threatening but nonetheless foreign to me. Mary, I began posting open letters to God and myself on the Internet—where literally the world could see it all. The Internet is so inundated with content, I didn't think many people would see my notes. I was wrong! Before I knew it, there were millions of people logging in from all over the world who could relate to the themes of my posts.

Then a publisher offered to help me take my gift to the next dimension by becoming an author. I decided to tell the story of how I discovered a gift worth treasuring buried under a mountain of insecurities. I wasn't sure what type of reaction to expect, but I was overwhelmed by it. I consider myself to be introverted, but I didn't mind sharing the highs and lows of my journey to encourage someone else who may be struggling.

Since I never thought that I'd add author to the list of my accomplishments, the entire process was a bit overwhelming. Flooded with all of the details that go into publishing, I was careful to guard the heart of why I began writing in the first place. I didn't become a writer for a book deal. I started writing to release my fears. When God helped me to remove the sources of those fears, new ones took their place. The day my book was released, my story was introduced to the world. If you haven't been able to tell by these letters, it's not the most angelic tale. I was stripped down to the core of my being with millions of eyes on me.

I was afraid.

I couldn't let that show, though, because I believed in the power of my truth. I used my vulnerability as a weapon and stood by my truth. Week after week I was introduced to legions of new people. Some of them were critics, a few of them were skeptics, but most of them were reflections of me. Like Dorothy, we were searching for our significance in an extraordinary world. Each time I sat down to an interview about the memoir I'd written, I felt like Dorothy crashing into a foreign world and dying to get home.

"That's how I feel when I'm away from you," I told my children as the movie played.

"That's how we feel when you're away," my son replied before my mouth could even close. His admission hit me like a ton of bricks. I tried to focus on the film, but my son had left me dumbstruck with his truth. I was so eager to return to the safety of our house that I never realized it wasn't home for them unless I was there. I would wait until the movie was over, but I wanted to explore his feelings a bit deeper. I watched Dorothy, intently hoping that following her steps would yield some form of revelation for me.

Dorothy meets many people as she ventures to find the road that will return her to family. Each of them has a frailty that has convinced them they will never amount to much.

As the story unfolds, we watch as each character unintentionally unearths the qualities they feel they lack. Their willingness to face their fears helps them realize the fears were never real to begin with. Dorothy eventually learns the key to returning home is simply just a click of her heels away.

While the movie was incredible, the opportunity I had to see life through my child's viewpoint was even more beneficial.

I believe at the heart of our most brilliant thoughts and desires is the fear that we don't have what it takes to bring it to fruition. I was most afraid that I would not be a good mom. My concern was rooted in the fact that I didn't personally have the resources or background to give my kids the life they deserved. Even though I was fearful, the launch of my book helped me to create a foundation of stability for my children. I was finally beginning to feel like a good mom, but my son's concerns weren't about material things. I was all he'd ever known, and he loved every bit of it. That was enough for him.

We both needed to be reassured that our worrying was in vain. I suggested that we share what makes us most afraid when we're apart. Not surprisingly, our fears were more alike than they were different. One of our mutual concerns was each other's safety when we were apart. Nothing dangerous has ever occurred when we've been apart, but there's a certain level of security that being together offers. We listed the various means of protection that existed around us until we eliminated any plausible areas of danger. Still, we acknowledged that there was a part of us that still felt like Dorothy. We realized that it really came down to missing one another.

I shared with him the power of your Son's parable and the lost sheep. I could tell he wasn't exactly sure how the two topics correlated, but I'm sure you can relate. No angel visited me when I was with child. I definitely wasn't a virgin, and there wasn't much cause for rejoicing. Yet the moment I realized I could feel my son kick inside of me, I knew that

God was real. It seemed implausible that a person could develop inside of me so quickly. Then I laid eyes on him and knew that God had trusted me with the most precious gift of all: life. Having an opportunity to mold, protect, and cherish a life is a precious trust given to us by God. When done with purity of heart and a desire to achieve excellence, it is the greatest investment of self one can give.

Having an opportunity to mold, protect, and cherish a life is a precious trust given to us by God. When done with purity of heart and a desire to achieve excellence, it is the greatest investment of self one can give.

I explained to Malachi that the point Christ was conveying is a testament of the love He has for us even when we've drifted from Him. He has promised to always come looking for us! There is no need to feel like Dorothy because our fears cannot separate us from the power of His love without our consent.

The same was true for the love I have for Malachi and Makenzie as their mother. I do not have a hundred sheep, as my field is plenty full with my two. I still felt the need to huddle my herd together and remind them of the constant blessing family offers. There will be many experiences that take us apart. Sleepovers, work, college, and travel are all realities we can't avoid. So we made a vow that night to choose love. Sure, there would be moments when we missed each other, but there's no harm in that. If we didn't miss each other, it would suggest that our presence did not add value. We can call one another, write a note, or send a text, but we will not invite fear into our love. If either of them forgets what I said and becomes the least bit lost, I guarantee I will be the mama shepherd that reminds them where they belong.

8

they're my do-over

"Woman, why do you involve me?" Jesus
replied. "My hour has not yet come."

John 2:4

*D*ear Mary,

My daughter, Makenzie, has the kind of smile that lights the room up. She doesn't just part her lips, clench her teeth, and say "Cheese." She opens her entire heart, grabs your soul, and lets you all the way in! Her arms stretch as wide as they can go before wrapping them around you with impressive force. No matter how many times you've experienced her hugs, the strength in her arms is a surprise you can't deny. At five years old, her arms have near perfect muscular definition. More times than I'd like to admit, I've caught her doing pull-ups on her bunk bed. Despite my insistence that she be careful, climbing on countertops and swinging from . . . well . . . anything is one of her favorite past times.

There's a saying that your kids will be "twice as bad" as you were as a child. The phrase is so commonly used that even before I had my son I used it frequently when engaging in conversation with an expectant mother. It was humorous until I was on the receiving end. I was on high alert, paying close attention to his behavior or attitude to determine if this would be true. I don't vividly remember being four or five, but I've heard some interesting stories, and to be frank, they're not great. If you let my older brothers tell it, my sister, Cora, and I couldn't be left alone for one minute. My sister and I are not even a full year apart in age. The age difference, or lack thereof, made us partners in mischief. I knew that we'd given our parents some adventures as teenagers, but the accounts of our childhood suggest that we were born with bold natures. My parents recount a story about my sister standing up in her crib as a baby and rocking back and forth in it until it broke into pieces. Evidently, it wasn't a one-time occurrence either. Three broken cribs later, they finally transitioned her into a less-fragile sleeping arrangement.

That's the beauty of youth, right? You get so caught up in the moment, you don't realize things are on the brink of falling apart while you're having fun. Maturity teaches you to slow down and look for the signs of weakness. Of course, I learned that lesson much later in life, because when I was Makenzie's age, swinging on the door of our bedroom was much more fun.

I can remember it now. My sister would watch as I balanced on the footboard of our bed. Once I was in position, she'd slowly swing the door in my direction until I could brace one foot on the doorknob, grasp the top of the door with my hands, and then bring the other foot to the other doorknob so that I was straddling the door. Then I'd use a leg to kick against the wall so that I'd swing toward the frame. Sometimes with the right balance of force, I could swing my leg for momentum and there would be no need to kick the wall each time. It was all fun and games until my mother stepped into the room. She wasn't nearly as amused with our shenanigans, but it was fun while it lasted.

I was just waiting for the day that I would find my son swinging from the ceiling fan or turning the bathtub into a wave pool. Malachi was too mild-mannered for that, though. I was confident that I had beaten the "twice as bad" curse.

I was ready to prepare dissertations on the illegitimacy of the claim, but I'm glad I held off. It gave me enough time to have a second thought: Makenzie. More and more lately, I'm beginning to wonder if there could be a slight bit of truth to the statement. As a parent, I straddle the line of admiration and complete terror when I witness her fearlessness in action. On nights when I call her down for dinner, it's not unusual for her to close her eyes and jump down the half flight of stairs—barely avoiding bumping her head—and not show even a morsel of fear. On the other side of the room, I'm holding my breath and bracing for the shriek of a five-year-old with a boo-boo! It never comes, and Makenzie is usually halfway through dinner before my breathing has resumed a normal pace.

So this is what I did?

I don't think anyone has sat her down and told her about my doorknob adventures—though I wouldn't put it past my mother to place a couple of seeds in her head. Assuming that didn't happen, my daughter somehow inherently became as spontaneous and adventurous as I had been with no coercion whatsoever.

Before Makenzie, I never fully understood why parents felt the need to become friends with their children. In the culture I was reared in, there was a very clear delineation between children and parents—separate tables when family came over, protocol when addressing adults, and consequences for failing to meet those standards are just a few of the rules I became accustomed to. Recognizing that my daughter is as calculated as she is audacious, I was beginning to wonder if staying on her good side—being the friend instead of disciplinarian—would ensure me an inside track to her future trickery. I didn't want to believe that "twice as bad" saying had any weight, but I wasn't sure if I could afford to be wrong.

I have witnessed an alternative to taking the friend route, though. I could become her warden. I could try to shut down everything, big and small, so that she realizes I'm constantly watching and prepared to punish every mistake she makes. Historically, many have justified such relentless punishment using Proverbs 13:24: "Whoever spares the rod hates their children, but the one who loves their children is careful to discipline them." But I was afraid that approach would strip her down to fear instead of caution. Or worse, she'd be counting down the days to her release from my home and then indulge in any and everything.

As parents, we hear conflicting truths about the right way to raise our children. There is much debate about proper forms of discipline. In the late 1960s, psychologist and researcher Diana Baumrind defined three styles of parenting: authoritative, authoritarian, and permissive. An authoritative parent is flexible and solves problems by collaborating with the child to confront behavioral challenges all while maintaining healthy affection. Authoritarian parenting takes a more direct approach and includes clear expectations and consequences, but shows minimal compassion. Lastly, the permissive parent shows an abundance of affection but provides little discipline.[1]

The authoritarian and permissive forms of parenting are widely considered less effective. But children don't come with a manual, and unless you stumble across Baumrind's research, you'd never know how to classify your specific style.

Later researchers added a fourth category: uninvolved parenting. This form of parenting has few demands, sporadic communication, and little sensitivity. While the basic needs of the child are still met, there is no real sense of attachment to the child's emotional and social development.[2]

I knew that no matter how busy my life became, I couldn't afford to become an uninvolved parent. But how involved should I be?

Makenzie's bravery is one of the things I love most about her. I only hope to teach her that there are some hurts she doesn't have to sign up for. Just because you can survive something doesn't mean you have to subject yourself to it. I need to make sure she isn't exposing herself to unnecessary duress just because she knows she can heal. I know many women who have discovered their ability to endure, but have yet to hone the ability to succumb to their vulnerability. It's a tricky thing when you train yourself to not even flinch when you feel like wailing. I became a master at it.

Just because you can survive something doesn't mean you have to subject yourself to it.

Fortunately, I found a way to recover, and I wanted my scars to spare Makenzie from as many wounds as possible. I'm not sure whether the "twice as bad" statement has validity or not, but I do know that if it holds any weight at all, she'll also be twice as good as I am. Perhaps we spend so long hoping our children don't inherit our flaws that we never consider the many strengths they could possess. Even more problematic than our own hopes, fears, and desires is never giving our children an opportunity

101

to bloom into the people God has purposed them to be. We pour many hopes and dreams into our children, but we can't allow those desires to be the paradigms by which we determine whether they're successful. We bring our children into the world, but God directs their paths. We're meant to aid them and give wisdom from our own steps, but we can't allow our desires to cloud their vision.

> *We bring our children into the world, but God directs their paths. We're meant to aid them and give wisdom from our own steps, but we can't allow our desires to cloud their vision.*

My prayer for Makenzie and Malachi is that they will fulfill all that God has predestined for their lives. I see so much of myself in their personalities, but I also see the unique traits that only God could impress. In John 14:12, Jesus tells Philip, "Whoever believes in me will do the works I have been doing, and they will do even greater things than these, because I am going to the Father." We have the same opportunity as Christ to become servants. By allowing God to become the center of our lives, we yield the way for our Master to take ultimate control.

The "twice as bad" notion scared me the most before I discovered there was so much more to me than my insecurities. I believe we become so afraid that our children will reflect our mistakes and issues that we unknowingly push them in that direction. If the only mold we use to form our children has been shaped by the negativity we've experienced, we limit the possibilities that exist for them. To suggest that our children will not have the option to be victorious and righteous in life suggests that we don't believe in the truth of God's Word.

Your womb was the gateway that allowed for the miracle of Christ's introduction into the world. You were trusted to create boundaries while His glory was developed and revealed. At the wedding in Cana, when the wine was gone but festivities continued, you were confident that the power of God that existed in Christ would be revealed. Though Christ did not feel His time had come, as His mother, you had an inside track to the awareness that the world was ready to receive His gift.

Without guidance from the Holy Spirit, there's no way that you could have known when and how to expose the greatness that existed in Christ. I remember the Scripture telling us that you were confused by Christ's reply when you found Him in the temple at the age of twelve. Young Jesus knew that He was being about His father's business, but God trusted you would help Him to establish limits. Yet eighteen years later, you were urging Him to reveal the mysteries you once kept in your heart. We don't always have to understand our children's actions to recognize the need for limits. You provided such a harmonious balance of discipline and nurture. As we witness the adult Jesus perform

If the only mold we use to form our children has been shaped by the negativity we've experienced, we limit the possibilities that exist for them.

103

His first miracle, one thing becomes supernaturally clear. Parenting is a never-ending job. There doesn't appear to be a promised day when our children no longer require the gentle nudging of wisdom telling them when to hold back or when to move forward.

I am learning that I can't be so concerned with their feelings that I cease to give them proper discipline. Nor can I be so consumed with discipline that I fail to understand that children become adults and must explore the world with boundaries on their own terms. Certainly we must shield, direct, and set restrictions as best as we can, but even our best efforts may yield results that leave us pondering whether or not we truly understand the child we've been given.

The reality is that our children themselves don't always understand the choices they make, no more than we understand some of our decisions. While I'm yet fine-tuning the method and approach I'll have with my children, I know for sure that I desire to give them the gift I see you gave your Son. You taught Him the discipline of knowing God's timing. Though Christ was doing His Father's work in the temple, it took time for Him to operate in that gift fully. We can become so excited about what's inside of us that we fail to allow it to fully develop.

Your commitment to protecting the development of Christ's grace is commendable, but even more courageous is having the discernment to recognize when His time had come. It's my prayer to be so sensitive to the spirit of my children that I recognize the difference between flat-out rebellion and the eager unveiling of the gifts God has placed inside of them. I will not become so consumed with who I think they must become that I fail to see who God has called them to be. May my heart be the diary that holds the clues I've witnessed along the way. As those clues take shape and begin to form the picture God is creating, I will be the gentle voice encouraging them to acknowledge when the fullness of their potential can be released.

9

too hurt to parent

"I have much more to say to you, more than you can now bear. But when he, the Spirit of truth, comes, he will guide you into all the truth. He will not speak on his own; he will speak only what he hears, and he will tell you what is yet to come. He will glorify me because it is from me that he will receive what he will make known to you. All that belongs to the Father is mine. That is why I said the Spirit will receive from me what he will make known to you."

John 16:12–15

*D*ear Mary,

As if the invention of films wasn't enough to keep us distracted, a more accessible form of entertainment was created: television. Since its inception there have been myriad types of programming offered. Accessible twenty-four hours a day, with literally thousands of diverse channels, it can be difficult to not become consumed with the plethora of options available on television. Over the course of the last couple of decades, much debate has been given to the benefits of the educational programming available to children. For many parents it has become routine to place their young children in front of the television so that they can begin to learn the fundamentals. Whether it's the alphabet, numbers, colors, or problem-solving, many networks have begun providing more education than entertainment in their lineup. Of course, it cannot replace the structure and personal connections our children experience in school.

In many cases it becomes a hindrance to the overall emotional and social development of children. Technology has made it difficult to master interpersonal skills. Instead of being a supplemental aid, it becomes the only influence they have. More pronounced than the attempts to educate are images that often demean women, glorify violence, and create premature curiosity about love, romance, and sex. Nielsen is a company that observes the behavior of consumers by studying what they watch and purchase. In 2014, Nielsen found that the average American adult spends more than five hours a day watching television.[1] If we combine that time with the demands of a full-time work schedule, plus the necessity of sleep, the twenty-four hours we have in one day dwindle significantly. There's very little time left for physical exercise or undivided personal interaction with family and friends.

I would venture to say that most people born in the television era are diligently striving to hone their time into something more productive. Still, many of us have guilty television pleasures in which we secretly indulge. Given the exorbitant amount of television consumption reported by Nielsen, I watch more than I would like to admit. I try to reason with myself that some programming offers me unprecedented insight into the human experience. The access helps me to determine how trauma and triumph shape a person.

There is a show that skillfully documents and challenges those experiences, called *Iyanla, Fix My Life*. On a recent episode she tackled the growing epidemic of fatherless children. By introducing her audience to a male guest who has thirty-four children by seventeen different women, she created a national dialogue about broken families.

I was instantly intrigued by the subject matter, but the patterns within these families made me take inventory of my own life. Having begun with a child out of wedlock and experiencing a divorce, my family fits squarely in the category of those from broken homes. The reality is that I could have avoided giving them that label by staying married, but they would have still been in a broken home. Not nearly as pronounced, but certainly as important is the fact that many people often end up seeking love in all of the wrong places. Those failed attempts at love often leave men and women with scars of shame that make them stop striving to become the best versions of themselves.

Especially when there are children studying our lives, we must understand the truth that even in our brokenness God granted us an opportunity for unconditional love. Every child, regardless of the circumstances surrounding his or her birth, is a gift of innocence and redemption. Unfortunately, they aren't always handled with care. We allow the shame and perception of others to taint our ability to offer them the attention and joy they so desperately need. Life comes to tempt us with fear and pride, but I believe parents teach children humility and grace. Too often our vision is blurred by the moments that have gone awry in our lives so that we no longer see our children clearly.

Failed attempts at love often leave men and women with scars of shame that make them stop striving to become the best versions of themselves.

I knew, especially as a teen mother, that there would be many negative opinions surrounding my son. Surely you experienced a similar situation as you watched Jesus begin His public ministry. Suddenly, He was no longer just your Son, your baby boy, but a grown man in the public eye. And clearly not everyone wanted to hear what Jesus had to say. He upset the establishment and overturned the expectations of how much God loves us and wants us to know and trust Him with our lives. In the Bible we're told how Jesus often

111

prayed to His Father and remembered that He was God's beloved Son. But I suspect Christ also carried your love for Him inside His heart as He faced the scrutiny and persecution from the haters and critics around Him.

Mary, I learn so much from your example. With my son and the negativity he elicits from some people, I truly only desire to make sure that he knows in spite of the circumstances his life holds incredible value. I never want his self-esteem to be marred by the judgment that he or I may receive. I wasn't sure why I felt so strongly about guarding him from those feelings or issues until I was watching the aforementioned television show.

As a single mother, my attention was centered closely on the mothers featured on the *Iyanla* show. I was intrigued by how they handled the fatherlessness their children experienced. It was my desire to learn from their challenges so that I could avoid some of the insecurities they experienced with their sons. The overwhelming consensus from the men who participated in the show was that their mothers had punished them for the sins of their fathers.

The women didn't realize how negatively it would impact their children, sons especially, to hear about the shortcomings of their fathers. The repeated derogatory statements made about their fathers taught the children to subconsciously reject a part of themselves. I've always tried to be positive when confronting the concerns and dilemmas my children had with their fathers, but I began to question whether I was truly doing a good job of it.

One of the challenges of communicating with your children is gauging what is emotionally age appropriate for their comprehension. It is even more difficult when television

112

attempts to answer many of the questions that plague their still-developing psyche. The more our children watch television and begin to connect with some of the very real life issues depicted, it becomes tough, if not impossible, to not identify with many of the feelings displayed. Eventually our kids begin to emulate what they've seen depicted on television. For instance, Makenzie began watching a television show on a station dedicated solely to children. I noticed that her attitude began shifting slightly, but initially I attributed it to age. She was becoming extraordinarily witty and charismatic. While those traits are certainly prominent in her personality, they started to grow exponentially and unnaturally as she watched this particular television show. I was becoming concerned about her behavior, but I wanted to identify the possible sources so that I could get to the root of the issue.

I'm almost sure the moment we give birth to our children an inner spy is also created. Mothers can become very creative when they need to get information about their children.

I sat down to watch the show with Makenzie. Whenever she laughed at a joke, I feigned ignorance and asked her what was funny. If she gasped at a dramatic moment, I asked her to recap what I missed. I understood the content of the show, but I wasn't sure how it was being perceived through her young eyes. As the episode was coming to an end, a character of Kenzie's same age came onto the screen. Within minutes of dialogue I understood just how similar Makenzie's personality was to the girl's. There was a notable difference, though. I wasn't the mother of the girl on the television show.

There were *many* mannerisms and expressions that were enjoyable for a viewing audience but would not be suitable should Makenzie desire to stay in my home. When the television show concluded, I very frankly asked Makenzie if she was trying to become the young girl featured on the show. She nodded her head and admitted that she thought the girl was funny, and she admired the attention she received.

I affirmed Makenzie in the unique personality that God had given her and encouraged her to be so confident that she didn't have to pretend to be someone she wasn't. There's nothing wrong with admiring someone's sense of self, but it should inspire you to enhance your own self-esteem, not to mimic his or hers. Of course, I had to communicate that in terms that she could understand at her age.

Fortunately, I was able to walk through that process with her. But what about the more difficult topics that threaten to rob the innocence of our children? In addition to television, the Internet is a dark and scary source of information. The unavoidable influence of both media makes rearing children frightening at best. I've become knowledgeable about parental controls and limited the consumption of television in my home to the weekends. Conversations about the slight or large similarities between their lives and those we see depicted on television are unavoidable.

There's nothing wrong with admiring someone's sense of self, but it should inspire you to enhance your own self-esteem, not to mimic his or hers.

As I watched *Iyanla*, I hoped that I would learn from the transparency of other mothers on how to handle the father voids in their lives. I learned that every truth doesn't require an elaborate explanation, and it certainly doesn't necessitate a battle. Multiple men appeared on the show with disenchanted views about women because of how their mothers communicated to them. One mother stated succinctly that her son had become a "container for her rage." Those closest to us experience the impact of our pain more than anyone else. Out of their heartbreak, they divulged unnecessary yet truthful details about their brokenness and disappointments. I can't say that I didn't have empathy for those women. I understood how such a thing could happen. I wasn't exactly sure how to share the painful reality of my own life with my children.

Explaining divorce, teen pregnancy, infidelity, and the scrutiny of being in a prominent family—among all the other unavoidable discussions about life—often left me searching for words. How can you explain the cause of a divorce when you're still processing it yourself? How can you satisfy their natural desire to question the whereabouts of the missing pieces in their lives when you haven't found your own? I couldn't explain in detail to my then two-year-old why her mother and father could no longer stay married. All I could offer her was that we both loved her very much and that we would be better parents if we were no longer husband and wife.

I knew that I had to say something, though, or else I'd be allowing the influence of television and friends to frame their perceptions. There was only one plausible option: prayer. I couldn't figure out the answer on my own. I wasn't sure I even trusted the answers I was beginning to formulate. It was through prayer that I was challenged to not unleash my bitterness on my children. I learned to protect my children from my healing process. For me, that meant actively making sure the process didn't become stagnant. We become experts at numbing ourselves in order to function—so much so that we never avail ourselves of the simultaneous healing that can occur while we persevere in spite of our pain. Our hurts were meant to be revealed to God, not unbridled on our innocent children.

Love requires the humility to admit when something is toxic, strength to not allow it to spread, and faith to heal the infection. I wanted to learn from the tears I witnessed the women on TV shedding, so I refused to allow for any bitterness or contempt in my heart. I removed myself and my children from the snares of toxic relationships and began to actively seek God's guidance in raising them. My fervent prayer became that Christ's truth expressed in John 16:12–15 would become my reality. Raising my children would require the Holy Spirit to come guide my every word and action. Watching Makenzie begin to transform into a character she saw on television made me realize that I may not know how outside influences may dare to affect the hearts and behavior of my children. Even scarier than that, I wasn't sure how their truth may dare to shape them. With God's help, I knew that I could muster the wisdom to guide and survive.

Love requires the humility to admit when something is toxic, strength to not allow it to spread, and faith to heal the infection.

Honestly, I always feared people who became so religious that they were no longer relatable to their searching children. I realize now the difference between relationship and religion.

Religion understands God as others perceive Him, but relationship is the intimate connection one actively pursues with Him. The cord that connects my heart with God's will is the Holy Spirit. Through the Holy Spirit I'm able to see and hear clearly the posture my heart must possess to minister uniquely to my children. Our lives become richer when we begin to invite the Holy Spirit into every aspect of our being. Balancing our natural inclination of anxiety and fear weigh heavily on us, and it's often difficult to remember to make Him our priority, but there is no greater reward.

Through the Holy Spirit I'm able to see and hear clearly the posture my heart must possess to minister uniquely to my children.

I know with certainty when my will has taken over and God's desire is on the proverbial back burner. Every area of my life begins to suffer when I don't put Him first. I know that I can't allow that to happen with my children. I didn't want to require the expertise of a television show host and a plethora of cameras to help me assess the damage. I wanted to avoid damage as much as possible. I hoped that my hunger and thirst for God's way in spite of my shortcomings would not just protect my children, but teach them as well. Effectively communicating on their level may not be my strongest suit just yet, but I learned a valuable lesson about truth from the life of Christ that I am passing down to my children.

There will be moments when there is much to say. Neither time nor wisdom may allow for a detailed explanation of where we are in life, but it doesn't have to barricade the truth.

117

Our truth is usually as simple as not being sure what's going to happen next, but knowing that God will direct our paths. The same Holy Spirit that has granted us access to the divine knowledge of God will also be available to our children when our words can no longer touch what only He can restore.

10

i need a village

"Why do you look at the speck of sawdust in your brother's eye and pay no attention to the plank in your own eye? How can you say to your brother, 'Let me take the speck out of your eye,' when all the time there is a plank in your own eye? You hypocrite, first take the plank out of your own eye, and then you will see clearly to remove the speck from your brother's eye."

Matthew 7:3–5

*D*ear Mary,

My sister's favorite pastime growing up was playing with dolls. Like most girls, I went through that stage as well, but I outgrew it swiftly as makeup, music, and fashion began to divide my attention. Cora had genuine interest in the different shapes, sizes, and lifelike similarities dolls could possess. The more detailed the dolls' faces were, the more she fell in love. As her fascination grew, my mother began gifting her with unique collector's item dolls. The human features, plush weight, and flexibility of the dolls truly resembled actual babies. I can remember many times in the store adults would stop to take a peek at the newborn baby with us. It was always humorous to see their faces when they realized they'd mistaken a doll for an infant. With the doll swaddled snuggly in newborn blankets and held close to her chest, it was very clear my sister was destined to be a great mother.

The only thing that gave her more excitement than the dolls was the opportunity to hold an actual baby. I, on the other hand, was quite the opposite! Babies were fun to hold for a few minutes, but the idea of actually having one with me all the time seemed like work. I enjoy children and definitely love my own, but what my sister has is something different. She doesn't have to have any previous connection with a baby to offer them a mother's love. I knew when I was expecting my son that she would be very eager to help with caring for him. I also knew that there would probably be more than a couple of times that I would have to remind her to give him back.

If I'm honest, I was insecure that she would take such good care of him that he would no longer want me as his mother. I felt that she would provide a level of nurturing to him that I was too ignorant to offer, and it scared me. I became overly territorial when he was just a few weeks old. I didn't want to risk exposing him to the expert knowledge she had.

It took only a couple months of sleepless nights for me to relinquish those fears. The truth is, I'm not sure I would have survived those times without her. What she offered me throughout the developmental years of my adolescence gave such credence to the saying "It takes a village to raise a child."

It would be several years after Malachi's birth before we learned my sister would face a battle with infertility. She would have to fight to receive a gift that so many take for granted. As heartbroken as she was when receiving the news, she wasn't dissuaded from her dreams. Her faith was activated with beautiful determination. She chronicles her journey with much more detail than I in her blog, *Fertility Faith*. There are few things more inspiring than her audacious tenacity to see her vision realized.

Our family has had few moments more joyous than when we learned my sister would become a mother. We welcomed my beautiful niece, Amauri, into our family via foster care. I'm not sure that any of us knew what to expect when she came. We desired to make sure she felt safe and protected in her new family. The moment I saw her, I picked her up and kissed her square on the cheek. As her aunt and godmother,

I wanted to make sure she knew me very well. I may have even encouraged her to pick me as her favorite aunt. I made sure to maintain my stature among very stiff competition.

Outside of the fact that Amauri was irresistibly lovable in her own right, I was eager to be an active part of my sister's village for her child. Considering how instrumental Cora was in helping me with Malachi, I wanted to give her a return on her investment. It truly sweetened the deal that my daughter, Makenzie, was Amauri's junior by only one year. They became instant playmates and fast friends. There may have been a point when my mother felt that having two girls so close in age was difficult, but having only one has its share of challenges too. You must become your child's playmate or they play alone. While imagination is healthy, it's not ideal for a child to spend significant time playing unaccompanied. Unfortunately, I no longer have the same energy as I did when I was swinging from doors, so Makenzie grows tired of me rather quickly.

There are many times when I'd rather be Makenzie and Amauri's ringleader rather than Makenzie's human jungle gym. Of course, my grace to be a ringleader lasts only a few nights before the two of them begin resembling my sister and me. Suddenly, being a human jungle gym no longer seems like such a bad gig. During the summer it's not uncommon for my sister and me to rotate evenings with the girls—after a few days of one home being filled with giggles while the other enjoys the tranquility of peace and quiet.

No one quite understands a mother like another mother. The challenges we must face in order to simply use the restroom, make dinner, take a bath, or build a career is like nothing I've ever faced before. As mothers, we allow our children into the most intimate crevices of our heart. The basic care of a child can be taught, but nothing fully prepares you for the undeniable love of holding your child. It can be difficult to welcome others into the nest we create for our children. Our insecurities can fool us into believing that the members of our village may be better equipped to mother than we are, but the reality is a mother's role is irreplaceable.

In the early 1900s, it was believed that the mystery of motherhood could be scientifically analyzed. Women began training in the area of "mothercraft." Cornell University pioneered a yearlong program to teach females the many aspects of domestic living. This course was designed to sharpen women's skills in the area of motherhood. The goal was to gauge how well students could manage household operations like budgeting, childcare, cooking, and more.

As mothers, we allow our children into the most intimate crevices of our heart.

In order to provide students with opportunities to practice their skills as parents, Cornell placed babies from orphanages and social service organizations into "practice houses" with the students. Under the supervision of a residential advisor, the first baby was placed in a home in 1919 and given the name Dicky Domecon (for "domestic economy"). The baby was cared for by eight students living in a campus apartment, supervised by a residential advisor. One girl would be responsible for the baby anywhere from seven to ten days before another classmate's shift would begin.

Once the babies were released for adoption, they were very popular among prospective parents because of the level of care they had received. It wasn't until fifty years later that the

124

program was removed from Cornell curriculum. Research revealed that though the basic needs of the babies were being met, the failure to establish a lasting bond might become more detrimental to the child in the long run.[1]

Decades later, there was curiosity about the actual babies used in the Cornell experiment. Attempts at locating one of the hundreds of babies used as subjects in this experiment proved to be very difficult. The curiosity proved too tempting for Lisa Grunwald, who authored *The Irresistible Henry House*, a novel that explored the potential emotional and psychological issues the children may have faced. In her book, she explores the challenges that the protagonist, Henry House, has as a result of being an infant in the program. The constant rotation of women caring for him as an infant created in him an inability to form a lasting bond with a mother figure. The missing connection in his life created commitment issues for him in romantic relationships.

The babies selected to live in the practice houses were there a year before being returned to the orphanages or social service departments they came from. While each case is different, we can assume that it may have taken quite a bit of time for some of the infants to create secure bonds in a stable home life. This is an unfortunate norm for many children raised in foster care systems around the country. When parents are unable to take care of their children, for any number of reasons, the children are placed in temporary living arrangements. These placements aren't always in the healthiest homes and sometimes leave the children more wounded than protected.

Our family commends my sister's commitment to provide a loving and safe environment for my niece, but we know that many children in the system never receive the safety they deserve. Their broken hearts leave them dependent on their own defenses and desperate to survive by any means necessary. While we may not be able to touch every broken child, we can become a village member for all the children we encounter. That's one of the things I've admired the most about my sister. She dutifully takes on the role of a village member for any child within her reach.

While we may not be able to touch every broken child, we can become a village member for all the children we encounter.

The "student mothers" involved in the Cornell program often took malnourished babies and nursed them back to health before returning them. We often avoid investing in people when we feel as though we can't offer them longevity, but no seed of love planted is a waste. Our ability to show grace and compassion to the children we meet on our journey is practice for the children we will eventually hold in our arms. When we don't agree with the parenting skills of our friends and family, we are too quick to judge and too slow to offer help. Why would we withhold perspective that could help someone become better?

If life has taught me nothing else, it has taught me to be slow to judge. As fascinating as the novel by Lisa Grunwald is, the truth is that you don't have to have been raised in an experiment to have psychological and emotional issues. We never know the path one is on when he or she begins the journey of parenting. The sad reality is that many of our friends and families may make choices and decisions as fathers and mothers that are difficult to comprehend. I've been guilty of having conversations about my concerns with other people instead of addressing them directly with the friend or family member involved. As my children begin to mature and confide in our family members about their emotions and feelings, I find myself thankful for those who have the wisdom to help me instead of judge me.

Helping to raise someone else's child requires wisdom. We must be sensitive to the role of the parent and compassionate toward the child. Good intentions without wisdom almost always end negatively. I have seen a few news stories of people spanking the children of strangers under the guise of helping them. While the child may have been exhibiting behavior that required adult attention, we cannot forget to combine wisdom and concern.

I do believe that it takes a village to raise a child, although I recognize that not every child is fortunate enough to be in a healthy village. I made a commitment to not be a part of the mob that runs broken children away. Whether a child stumbles into my reach or is born in my circle, if it is possible to help, I will. I truly need to practice sowing those seeds so that I can reap them in my own children. It is my hope that when my children grow numbingly familiar with the sound of my voice

It is my hope that when my children grow numbingly familiar with the sound of my voice or cadence of my chastisement, someone in their lives will offer perspective that helps them see more clearly.

or cadence of my chastisement, someone in their lives will offer perspective that helps them see more clearly. I cannot desire that unless I am willing to sow it.

All mothers have moments when we encounter someone else's child. We are faced with the decision to help them find their way or to laugh while they stumble. We must remember that our children will have their own steps to take and paths to survive, and be as gentle and kind with others as we hope someone will be with our own.

Your Son so beautifully questioned the way we choose to see the world in Matthew 7:3–5. It challenged me to stop pointing a finger at what others could do better and instead rise to the occasion of actively practicing love, not judgment.

11

ends don't meet

Jesus sat down opposite the place where the offerings were put and watched the crowd putting their money into the temple treasury. Many rich people threw in large amounts. But a poor widow came and put in two very small copper coins, worth only a few cents. Calling his disciples to him, Jesus said, "Truly I tell you, this poor widow has put more into the treasury than all the others. They all gave out of their wealth; but she, out of her poverty, put in everything—all she had to live on."

Mark 12:41–44

*D*ear Mary,

I've been handling the incredible task of preparing for an out-of-state move. The days have begun to blur together as the demands of work, parenting, and my personal life begin to collide. The final stretch has been the most difficult. I've been trying with great diligence to remain within the budget allotted for my family. Being more conscious of the added expenses a move will require has naturally made me pay closer attention to my discretionary spending. After a divorce that left me with a couple hundred dollars to my name, I've been fortunate enough to provide a stable middle-class lifestyle for my two children. It was not without struggle that I came to learn and understand the value of a dollar. Hardly anything prepares you for the demands of creating and implementing a budget like being faced with the reality that your children's well-being is on the line.

I was adamant about gaining full independence from my parents at the earliest age possible. I quarreled and struggled with them for the right to be free. It took gaining that independence for me to recognize they weren't trying to control me; they were hoping to protect me. I became so focused on engaging in battle with them that I didn't realize they were preserving my dependence until I was prepared to fully take care of myself. They knew I wasn't ready, but I had too much pride to admit they were right.

If I could do things all over again, I would have stayed in the safe haven of innocence for much longer than I did. I was too hungry for control of my own life, so I took matters into my own hands. It took less than thirty days for me to realize that I wasn't nearly as prepared as I thought I was. I took a crash course in domestic economy when I moved out of my parents' home and began living with my boyfriend. With no job experience or notable achievements in education outside of high school, the options for careers were limited to entry-level minimum-wage jobs.

The competition for employment in those fields was overwhelming. The backgrounds behind the anonymous faces in the interview waiting rooms could not be revealed, but our eyes all held a familiar look: desperation. I knew within a couple of days we would be receiving an eviction notice at our apartment. We had no source of income that could dissuade the apartment management from following through with the notice. I expanded my search from jobs with biweekly checks to opportunities where I could make cash quickly. I wanted to prevent the various warnings of service disconnections piling up in our mailbox from becoming promises.

I had far too much pride to admit my circumstance to my parents. I wasn't sure that they'd even be willing to help me after the multiple chances they'd given me to avoid the path I was currently on. There was no way I could be selective about the opportunities I needed to generate income fast. I sacrificed a piece of my dignity and began waitressing at a club where women removed their clothes for money.

Although I was able to use the cash to pay our bills, I must admit that a part of me was ashamed that providing for my son became contingent on whether a man was attracted to my smiling face or intrigued by my flirtatious banter. My story is not a unique one, but the proximity to financial stability was a blessing I took for granted. The rising percentage of unemployment and poverty has become an unavoidable concern for many Americans. In 2013, approximately 45.3 million people were living below the poverty line.[1] The simplest definition of the poverty threshold is the minimum level of income deemed suitable for a family living in a particular country. The prevalence of poverty can be easily measured in numbers and percentages, but there's nothing like giving this serious reality a face.

The strength of our economic future has become more and more bleak each year. The dwindling middle class has created an alarming disparity between the upper and lower classes. Scarier than the number of families struggling to make ends meet is the unfortunate belief that the dilemma will continue on for generations. Families are no longer interested in offering their children hope that a better tomorrow awaits them. Frankly, they're too consumed with the struggle to survive today. Couple that with the education available to children living in poverty-stricken communities, and success becomes an anomaly and recurrent poverty the norm.

When Katrina Gilbert allowed cameras to document her life as a single mother, she did not realize how close she was to destitution. It wasn't until she began watching the finished documentary—called *Paycheck to Paycheck*—that she saw her life from the outside looking in. She was not impressed with the view. For Gilbert and her three children, the $18,000 a year she brought home failed to meet the requirements of basic care and provision. Viewers watched as she struggled to choose between purchasing her medication or having food in the pantry for her children. It became increasingly clear as the film progressed that her survival was nothing short of miraculous. According to U.S. Department of Health & Human Services, in 2013 a family of five would need to make $27,570 to avoid the poverty classification.[2] The discrepancy of more than $9,000 a year may be nominal in some minds, but it would make an extreme difference for Gilbert's family.

It has been two thousand years since your time here on earth, Mary. The innovation of technology and development of economic power has brought much change to the world, but it has not changed the unfortunate reality of poverty for many families. While some mothers dream of sending their children to great colleges, others hope they'll be able to scrounge enough money to prepare a decent meal. The guilt associated with not being able to give your children the best can be tormenting. In a materialistic society, sending children to school with well-worn shoes and without the latest fashions creates tragic opportunities for intimidation by other students. As trivial as shoes and clothes may be compared with food and shelter, we all desire to give our children the best start possible.

Christ's birth was unconventional for a plethora of reasons. Were you ever disappointed that you weren't able to give Him a normal childhood? As if the fact that He was born in a stable wasn't unusual enough, the early part of His life was spent hiding from King Herod, who desired to kill all the boys born in Bethlehem. I can't imagine the honor you must have felt being entrusted with the life of Christ.

How did you release your image of how most babies were raised in order to embrace the differences your family faced? There may have been a part of you, like most mothers, that wanted to raise Him with as much stability as possible. So much of our worth as parents is often placed on our ability to provide structure for our children. Unfortunately, we don't always have access to the materials necessary to ensure stability.

The guilt associated with not being able to give your children the best can be tormenting. We all desire to give our children the best start possible.

I've studied the lives of many thought leaders from history. The backgrounds of our most prolific artists, theologians, businesspeople, and entertainers vary significantly. Some of them were born with abundant resources, while others have experienced much more humble beginnings. I wanted to determine if there was a specific formula I could instill in my children.

I studied the life of great inventors like Benjamin Franklin. He was the fifteenth of seventeen children born to a candlemaker. He was able to receive only two years of formal education and had to supplement what he missed by reading as many books as possible. Franklin moved out on his own at the tender age of seventeen. He founded a prosperous printing company that gave him the opportunity to retire early and dedicate time to his other interests. Thanks to his creativity and determination, not his economic circumstances, he became responsible for many inventions we continue to use more than three hundred years after his birth.

I explored the life of Frederick Douglass, who was born into slavery but committed to educating himself by any means necessary. When his master's wife was chastised for teaching him the alphabet, he began gathering whatever written material he could find and continued teaching himself. In 1838 he escaped from the chains of slavery and became a prominent voice as an abolitionist and author. In 1888, he was the first African American to receive a vote to become president. He was born a slave but died a well-respected leader.

Every child deserves the opportunity to witness their parents making the best out of what life has offered them.

My son recently received an assignment to do a report on the life of a historical figure. For his assignment he chose to focus on Maya Angelou. A well-respected poet and nominee for the esteemed Pulitzer Prize, she held a concrete position as a literary giant. It wasn't until my son's report, however, that I learned of her past. By the age of seventeen, Angelou worked as a prostitute and then eventually became a madam. Her life certainly encouraged millions of people to live their best life, but her wisdom did not come without struggle.

There are countless stories of phenomenal people whose names we may never know. The one commonality that exists between all the greats is the commitment to give their best. Had they dared to allow their circumstances to dictate their future, they would have been limited to dreaming within their means. The world would have been robbed of the ingenuity and pioneering efforts of countless individuals.

136

Perhaps our true wealth lies not in our bank accounts but in the mindsets we confront our issues with. The number of shoes our children possess will not determine their success, but the steps they take to become better people and citizens will be the most important scale of all. As a mother who has been very transparent about my journey, I can identify with the feelings Katrina Gilbert expressed in the post-interview after seeing her documentary. There are many moments throughout the film when she could not shield her children from the reality of their financial inconsistency.

I pray that when her children, or mine, are given the opportunity to see their lives through the eyes of their mother, they will recognize our mutual truth: We're giving them the best we have. Every child deserves the opportunity to witness their parents making the best out of what life has offered them. Matthew 25:21 teaches us that if we're faithful over a few things, God will put is in charge over many things. Everyone's allotment of "few" may be different, but there are no limits on what faithfulness can do.

The story of the widow's offering in Mark 12 taught me that sacrifice has nothing to do with an amount and everything to do with the heart from which it is given. We must trust that just as Christ recognized the woman who gave from her poverty, He sees our hearts. The inventors and trailblazers who made history prove that one idea can change the trajectory of our lives. There are millions of

I hope that my tenacity to overcome my circumstances paves a path for my children to excel beyond what I accomplish.

137

mothers struggling with the concept that they don't have much to give their children. As they continue to move forward with relentless determination, I hope they progress with peace. May their confidence reside in the truth that they've given their best, and may their determination inspire them to never quit. The effects of rumor and peer pressure are undeniable, but a relentless spirit has more strength than the two combined. I hope that my tenacity to overcome my circumstances paves a path for my children to excel beyond what I accomplish.

Mary, surely your example paved the way for Jesus to enter into the fullness of His identity as God's Son on earth. You surrendered your life to God so that you could give life to this Savior for the world. You demonstrated what it means to give your life to God in service to others, reminding us all to do the same as we look to your precious Son for our hope.

12

from joy to grief

"Your brother will rise again. . . . I am the resurrection and the life. The one who believes in me will live, even though they die; and whoever lives by believing in me will never die. Do you believe this?"

John 11:23, 25–26

*D*ear Mary,

On December 14, 2012, in Newtown, Connecticut, the family members of twenty-seven people were thrust into the national spotlight. The buzz of the holiday season was halted when a tragic school shooting occurred and resulted in the death of twenty children and six adults. Unable to fully comprehend their grief, family members began publicly memorializing the lives of their children. In hopes of diverting the attention from their violent deaths, their families focused on the joy their short lives offered. An understandably emotional Richard and Krista Rekos sat down for a television interview three days following the shooting in their small town. Their six-year-old daughter, Jessica, was one of the twenty children who lost their lives that cold day. The couple conveyed to the reporter that talking about their Jessica "brings tiny moments of comfort."[1]

In 2012, the population of Richard and Krista's town was a quaint 27,560. The Rekos knew their town well, but on the day news of a shooting spree began to circulate, it felt like a different place. Camera crews from around the world piled into the picturesque Connecticut town to report about the second deadliest shooting at a school in the history of the United States. Krista recounted her reaction when she was made aware of the terrifying news: "I was running, and I just kept thinking, 'I'm coming for you, honey, I'm coming.'"[2]

Parents who began crowding the local fire station were given information piece by piece. They were notified that many of the students, teachers, and staff were taking cover inside Sandy Hook Elementary while law enforcement attempted to capture the assailant. It wasn't until after one p.m. that afternoon that the families of the twenty-six victims learned that they would have to begin the heartbreaking procedure of making funeral arrangements.

I'm not sure there is anything more difficult to process than death. The painful truth that we will never again hold dearly cherished loved ones leaves us with many unanswered questions. While I have experienced grief in varying degrees in losing grandparents, uncles, and even friends, I'm almost sure that nothing compares with burying a person you gave life to. Sequestered in the back of every parent's mind is a fear too grave to ever place into words. The possibility that one day life could force you to give an unscheduled good-bye to the person you waited nine months to say hello to is impossible to comprehend.

News coverage recounted the events of that day in harrowing detail. It took only a matter of moments for the name of the suspect, Adam Lanza, to be released. Law enforcement and news agencies conducted numerous investigations into Lanza's mental mindset and searched for any possible motives for the crime. Courageous families invited the public into their grieving process, and as a nation we stood in disbelief at how a normal day could become so catastrophic. I remember watching and admiring the resolution of the families to be strong in spite of what I imagined was insurmountable pain.

Suddenly my children's small annoyances I complained about no longer mattered. Their rooms were a mess, they

didn't always remember their homework, and I often wondered if I needed to get their hearing checked. They were
still my babies, though, and they were still here. I'm not sure
there is a definition of devotion more fitting than that of a
mother to her child. Before we ever feel the flutters of life
moving in our wombs or know the gender of the fetus nestled
inside of us, our instinctive protective nature kicks in. The
moment we learn of our pregnancy, everything shifts—from
our eating habits to the clothes we wear. Our every thought
is centered on creating an environment where our children
can be comfortable with growing at their own pace.

So protective are the hearts of mothers that many wait
until the beginning of their second trimester of pregnancy
to share the news of their gestation. Fear of a miscarriage
or a complication in development convinces many women
to treasure the news of their pregnancy in their heart before
sharing it with the world. According to the American Pregnancy Association, anywhere from 10 percent to 25 percent
of clinically recognized pregnancies end in miscarriages.[3]
Even at the conservative end, that's one in ten pregnancies.
A miscarriage is most likely to occur within the first thirteen
weeks of pregnancy. I remember bubbling with excitement
at the news of my daughter, but also being selective with
disseminating information. I was concerned that my body
might reject the pregnancy and I would be forced to issue a
painful retraction.

Once I was out of the danger zone for miscarrying, the
relief I felt was replaced with fear of having a stillborn or
going into premature labor. There were many moments I
had to actively remind myself to live in the moment instead
of focusing on the painful possibilities of my excitement

coming to an end. I'm not sure if this happens with everyone, but it felt like the moment I learned I would be giving birth, the more inundated I was with news of pregnancies ending tragically and abruptly. I remained cautiously optimistic until I held my babies in my arms.

It took only a couple of months after having my children for me to forget what life was like before them. Each moment our eyes lock it feels as though I loved them long before they were conceived. It doesn't take long for mothers to build their lives around their children. Bedtimes, homework, and curfew can determine the entire course of our week. Children are as consuming as they are rewarding. Playing an active role in the growth and development of who they will become requires unprecedented attention. Our lives are the gravity of their universe, and we diligently strive to properly hold them down.

It doesn't take long for mothers to build their lives around their children. Children are as consuming as they are rewarding.

When we are finally past the finish line of labor, the marathon of rearing our children begins. Through their infancy, childhood, adolescence, and even through adulthood, our minds are flooded with concerns about their past, present, and future. I know that I spent far less time worrying about the possibilities of losing them as I did being anxious about how to raise them. But stories about devastating school shootings like the one that occurred at Sandy Hook Elementary demand that we not become so overwhelmed with the logistics of raising our children that we forget to enjoy them. Tears streamed nonstop down my face as I imagined the pain those parents were feeling. What had begun as a routine day quickly took a turn for the worst.

I'm not sure if giving birth to God's Son lessened or intensified contractions, but I bet having an idea of when they were coming would have been beneficial for you. Several centuries after Christ was born, the field of medicine merged with technology. The merge allowed for inventions of machines like a cardiotocograph, which made it easier to assist birthing mothers. The machine uses sensors placed against the mother's abdomen to record the fetal heartbeat and uterine contractions and prints out a strip of paper that shows a record of the activity.

When I was in labor with my son, Malachi, I watched the paper strip constantly. The nurse explained which line showed contractions and which showed the rate of his heartbeat. After only an hour or so, I'd become an expert at reading the machine. I knew when a contraction was coming and ending. The paper strip that began stacking neatly by my bedside had peaks with valleys of all different shapes and sizes. As labor progressed the peaks became closer and the valleys smaller, but they did not go away fully until my son's last push out of the womb.

Each child brings his or her own set of peaks and valleys that we must face, but as our heart expands to love each child, so does our tenacity and strength to climb those mountains. Certainly, there is fear with each climb. We may often question our strength and ability to fully make it to the top. Though the fear of failing our children may haunt us, the temptation to quit on our children evades us. What incredible disappointment one must experience when they can no longer fight because their child does not live!

How did you handle the view of the cross that held your Son on Calvary?

While many mourned the loss of their Savior, you were stricken with the anguish of not being able to spare your Son's life. In my culture it's not uncommon to hear a mother tell her child, "I brought you into this world, and I'll take you out!" Of course, the saying isn't an actual threat of death, but rather a reminder that no matter how adult our children may become, there is a level of respect we're to be given because we gave them life. Failure to yield that respect will not result in physical death, but perhaps some of the support, wisdom, hopes, and pleasures that come from a mother will no longer be accessible. That method of intimidation has been used for as long as I can remember. But what becomes of the mother who brought her child into the world and would do anything to bring him or her back?

When I began sharing my story on my blog, I was overwhelmed by the response of people from all over the world. Initially I thought that I was writing about infidelity, insecurities, hope deferred, and dissipating faith. It wasn't until my path crossed with Wendy Kitter's that I learned differently. She began commenting and writing on my page as the entries began speaking directly to her. Wendy wasn't aware of the details occurring in my personal life, nor did I have knowledge of the experiences that led her to identifying with my pain. It wasn't until we began sending letters to one another in a more private medium that I learned I wasn't just blogging to people with stories identical to mine. I was sharing about the nondiscriminatory reality of heartbreak.

Wendy shared with me that she had lost her daughter, Adriel, at the tender age of four in a tragic accident. Wendy stumbled across my blog, where I was asking God the very question she was holding in her heart: "Why?"

While I cannot compare the pain of my experiences with Wendy's sorrow from losing a child, it did help me to realize that the emotions surrounding heartbreak are similar for all of us. As my blog began to take on a life of its own, I was confronted with the necessity of treating the ache emitting from my heart. How would I use the influence of my pain to become a better person? I asked myself. I was beyond consumed with fear, and I began to doubt if the reservoir of hope I once believed in truly existed. As I began to explore my own need to heal, I realized that hope isn't a location, it's a mindset.

Foolishly, we trick ourselves into believing that there is a certain set of accomplishments we must complete and accolades we must receive before we can overflow with hope. Then when life's failures and disappointments hold us captive, we experience drought. In John 11, when your Son finally arrived to visit Martha and Mary, their brother, Lazarus, had been in the tomb for four days. When news spread that Jesus was on the way to comfort them, Martha ran into town to meet Him. Mary, however, opted to stay home by her brother's tomb. When Jesus was outside of their house, an emotional Mary went outside to meet Him. "Lord, if you had been here, my brother would not have died," she said.

Mary's heart was broken because her hope had been in Christ's coming earlier to spare her brother's life. Though Christ performed a miracle that brought Lazarus back to life, not everyone's story has that type of ending. God doesn't answer our prayers based on our demands, because He knows the route we must travel to do His will. I wondered what consolation one could receive when faced with the challenge of saying good-bye.

The words Christ spoke to Martha before He even made it to their home resonate deeply within me. "The one who believes in me will live, even though they die; and whoever lives by believing in me will never die" (John 11:25–26). I've heard that Scripture recited at funerals for as long as I can remember, but the depth of its meaning wasn't always clear to me. Then I realized that beyond the initial reference to eternal life, our lives as believers have the potential to reap a harvest long after we've joined our Father in heaven. When we live a devoted life to Christ, our additions to the world cannot be erased even though our heart no longer has rhythm.

Not many people will have the opportunity to say that God actually brought a relative back to life, but they do have an opportunity to transform their grief into power. That's exactly what Candy Lightner did. The mother of three had three encounters with drunk drivers. Driving with her eighteen-month-old twin daughters, Serena and Cari, in the car, Candy was rear-ended by a drunk driver. Serena was covered in bruises and multiple cuts from broken glass. Six years later, an unlicensed driver who was under the influence of tranquilizers struck Candy's son, who required several surgeries to repair his broken bones and suffered permanent brain damage.

The accident on May 3, 1980, would be the final straw for Candy. Her daughter Cari, now thirteen years old, was headed to a church carnival when she was hit and killed by a drunk driver. Four days later in the den of her home, Candy created an organization named MADD, Mothers Against Drunk Driving. "I promised myself on the day of Cari's death that I would fight to make this needless homicide count for something positive in the years ahead," Candy expressed. Though her daughter was no longer physically with her, the memory of her life has touched millions.

The mothers I've written about in this letter, and countless others who've battled with a sea of grief, have one commonality. They could not simply accept that their children's lives came to an end. Whether through sharing their stories on news outlets, climbing a mountain in Peru, finding comfort in a blog, or spurring a movement that creates change, these mothers have enabled their children to live on through their memories. I did not have the chance to meet the beautiful children that brought these families so much joy, but because of their moms, I know their names.

God trusted you to suffer because He knew the great destiny waiting to be revealed on the other side of your tears.

Christ may not have come in the timing that Mary and Martha had hoped, but He knew long before He arrived that Lazarus would live again.

I presume that one of the difficulties with managing grief isn't knowing when the aching may fade, because it may never fully disappear. Perhaps the challenge is *how* the memories of our loved ones will live on long after they're gone. I told my dear friend Wendy that Adriel's life has inspired me to hug my children tightly and express my love each moment I can. She will live on in the kisses, laughs, and joy I share with my children.

Mary, you have no idea how your Son's life has continued to live on in the hearts of billions. Having to view your Son nailed to the cross until the last breath escaped His body must have felt like your own death. I really need you to know that the pain you experienced was not in vain. God trusted you to suffer because He knew the great destiny waiting to be revealed on the other side of your tears. I'm grateful that the love of a mother cannot be confined by a grave.

13

i don't have a mom

"You're familiar with the old written law, 'Love your friend,' and its unwritten companion, 'Hate your enemy.' I'm challenging that. I'm telling you to love your enemies. Let them bring out the best in you, not the worst. When someone gives you a hard time, respond with the energies of prayer, for then you are working out of your true selves, your God-created selves. This is what God does. He gives his best—the sun to warm and the rain to nourish—to everyone, regardless: the good and bad, the nice and nasty. If all you do is love the lovable, do you expect a bonus? Anybody can do that. If you simply say hello to those who greet you, do you expect a medal? Any run-of-the-mill sinner does that."

Matthew 5:43–47 THE MESSAGE

*D*ear Mary,
   I have a friend who made a decision to never, ever have children! I'm not one of those mothers who feels every woman should experience the miracle of childbirth. I recognize the responsibility and demands of being a mother should be taken very seriously. If a woman adamantly feels like she should not embark on the journey of motherhood, I don't try to convince her otherwise.

When my friend first began declaring her womb would be child-free, I wanted to warn her that my mother had said something very similar. Five children later, though, she had to eat those words. But I remained silent and let my friend continue to spout about her independence from babysitters. I never saw any problem with it and even shared my jealousy that she could sleep in without interruption. Who am I to tell her how to live her life? But when my friend told me that her unwillingness to have a child was beginning to take a toll on her marriage, I found myself torn. Based on how she was relaying her husband's sentiments, it seemed to be very important to him that she be willing to at least consider his feelings in the matter.

I was worried that the disagreements they were experiencing were growing in frequency and intensity. "Why can't he just accept that I don't want to be a mother?" She was growing frustrated, and I was becoming concerned that their inability to compromise would create future resentment.

I realized that I'd heard her say she didn't want to be a parent repeatedly, but I never investigated *why* she didn't want to become one. So I asked. After hearing a laundry list of reasons why she didn't feel ready, I noticed one theme at the core of each explanation: fear. She was afraid she would have a strong-willed child. She was afraid that her husband wouldn't know how to handle her during pregnancy. She was afraid that since her mother had passed away, she would have no reference on how to be a great mother.

When she finally mentioned the last one, I recognized how daunting it must be to become a mother when your own mother can't offer support. I was really taking my mother for granted! Whenever the kids had a cold, I called my mother before I called the doctor. If the children had a conflict with a teacher at school, I asked my mother how to handle it. On the many nights when the children's behavior began to resemble an unnamed creature from a horror story, I confided in my mother. She was my go-to resource on how to handle the stress of motherhood.

When I confronted my friend with my suspicion that her reasons for not wanting to have a child were all based in fear, she took a minute to think. "I guess you're right," she admitted. When we begin to allow our actions and decisions to be dictated by our fears, we ultimately lose sight of the power of God. His Word teaches us that He has not given us the spirit of fear. Yet many of us grow comfortable living in the confinement our worries create. I challenged my friend to at least be open to the truth that God is capable of making a provision for her journey should she become a mother.

For me, it would have been different if her reasoning for not having a child were rooted in a belief that God had not placed the desire for a child in her heart. But she admitted there were moments she truly considered having a child. She quickly vanquished those desires with fears and then began forcing her decision on her husband. We ended our lunch that day with her making me a promise. I asked her if she would at least be open to the possibility of truly hearing from God, not fear, about becoming a mother. Though she was reluctant, she ultimately agreed.

I think she was afraid that she was going to have to confront the reality that she had not truly filtered her decision through the Holy Spirit.

Many of us grow comfortable living in the confinement our worries create.

Isn't it interesting how we make a list of things we absolutely will not do, but then tell God He has complete control over our lives? We cheat on God when we choose to have an affair with our fear. When Jesus was walking in the street in Judea, a man came to Him asking what he must do to receive eternal life. After Christ admonished him to keep the commandments given to Moses, the man told Him that since his youth he'd done that. When your Son upped the ante and then challenged the man to sell whatever he owned, give it to the poor, and follow Him, the man became discouraged.

While the man held on to His possessions, God taught the disciples a valuable lesson. Those who "have it all" will have difficulty inheriting the kingdom. Matthew 19:24 states, "It is easier for a camel to go through the eye of a needle than for someone who is rich to enter the kingdom of God." I remember when I "turned" my life over to God. I gave Him specific instructions about what must happen. When He moved too slow or didn't do what I desired, I took matters into my own hands.

We cheat on God when we choose to have an affair with our fear.

I didn't want my friend to experience the detours my life made. Whether or not she had a child was inconsequential to me, but her understanding the humility required to truly serve God meant more to me than anything. Above all things I desired her to have the peace of knowing that, should God place the desire of motherhood in her heart, He would guide her through the process. I couldn't help but remind her how blessed she was to have an example of a mother—in the form of her memories—that she wanted to model.

Michelle had a much different story. Although Michelle's mother had her when she was an adult, she did not feel prepared to become a mother. If you let Michelle tell it, her mother was too selfish to sacrifice her fun for responsibility. Michelle's mother was in and out of her life, so Michelle lived with her aunt into her teens. Though her mother never fully explained what kept her from being in her daughter's life, Michelle's aunt suspected she was struggling with a drug issue. Unfortunately, her aunt would not live to see whether or not her suspicion was true—she died unexpectedly. After spending most of her life in the stability of her aunt's home, Michelle was forced to live with her mother and her current boyfriend.

Michelle is naturally beautiful and always has been. She was the first of her classmates to develop and fill out her womanly curves. Her teenage face remained remarkably clear and blemish-free, while her friends' started to mirror slices of pizza. Potential dates lined up to ask Michelle out. She took it all in stride, though, too focused on her education to give a second thought to the attention she received. Her future was more important to her than romance. Unfortunately, her mother did not share in that wisdom. It was almost as if she saw her as competition. She would demean Michelle about everything, from her looks to her future, in front of her friends. Michelle learned to pretend that she had grown accustomed and immune to her mother's verbal abuse.

When Michelle learned she'd been awarded a full scholarship to a university a thousand miles away, it was cause for celebration. It seemed evident that she needed to be away from the toxic environment of her home. Her hard work and dedication had finally paid off. Soon her life morphed into a story fit for a fairy tale. Michelle found her soul mate at college, and the two got married shortly after graduation. It was only a matter of time before she began to create the kind of family she always wanted growing up.

Thanks to the world of social media, news of Michelle's pregnancy made it back to her mother, who reached out to her. It had been years since they'd spoken. There was quite a bit of dysfunction in their relationship that hadn't yet been dealt with, but Michelle's mother was hoping to make amends and move forward.

Needless to say, this did not go over well. Venting on the phone to friends who knew her history, Michelle expressed her frustration with the utter gall of her mother.

How do you convince someone to not be angry when she has every justifiable reason to be upset? In Matthew 5, when your Son was with His disciples and a crowd had gathered, He began to teach about many different things, but the lesson that I gleaned the most from focused on loving our enemies. I must admit that of all His teachings, this is the one that is most challenging for me. I consider myself to be a forgiving person, but there have been a few times when I know that I didn't rise to the challenge to show love. I tried to apologize, but there were some friendships that couldn't survive the damage that my pride had done.

There are few generational lessons more important than maintaining a clean heart and learning the beauty of forgiveness.

In Michelle's case, regardless of what she verbalized to her friends, there was still a little girl inside of her hoping to be loved by her mother. We *all* have difficulties when it comes to loving our enemies. Of course, Michelle shouldn't subject herself to the verbal abuse she had once endured, but if her mother had truly made a change for the better, Michelle could have a chance to see a side of her she'd only dreamed of knowing.

God is capable of softening the most hardened hearts. Becoming a mother when your mother hasn't been ideal or is no longer accessible to you must be trying. While you can never recover the time that has been lost, keeping your heart open to the possibilities of love and growth is important. Relationships take work and require reciprocation.

We can't compare the legitimacy of our relationships with those we see around us. Every connection in our life has its own unique identity. We must release ourselves from the belief things must go our way and allow God to open our hearts. Michelle and her mother may never have daily conversations about the many facets of their lives, but Michelle can choose to forgive and love. One day her child may have a complaint against her, but there are few generational lessons more important than maintaining a clean heart and learning the beauty of forgiveness.

Mary, you surely had to deal with forgiveness if you were present to watch as your Son's life drained from His body on the cross. How excruciating it must have been for you to see Him so tortured and mistreated, so misunderstood and manhandled. He endured the ultimate injustice to save the rest of the world, including you. But I'm guessing you would have done anything in your power to save Him in those moments when the Roman soldiers were piercing His hands and feet with iron spikes, hammering Him into those beams of wood.

14

moms hide in the bathroom

"Here's what I want you to do: Find a quiet, secluded place so you won't be tempted to role-play before God. Just be there as simply and honestly as you can manage. The focus will shift from you to God, and you will begin to sense his grace."

Matthew 6:6 THE MESSAGE

*D*ear Mary,
I found the perfect hideaway for when life becomes too overwhelming. I must admit it took some time for me to find a place to just breathe without the stress of doing something for someone. Don't get me wrong—I love my children with all of my heart. I have an incredible calling that allows me to truly serve people. I'm grateful for every moment of my day. I know for sure there was a time when I wasn't so fortunate, when I was simply going through the motions of life. There were momentary pockets of happiness, but I had no real joy.

Since then so much in my life has changed. I had an encounter with your Son that changed everything I understood about life, growth, and grace. The moment I began to take the steps He'd ordered without asking questions, I experienced revolutionary change in my life. I sought His direction before making plans. I became anxious for nothing but His ultimate will for my life. Of the many blessings He's bestowed since I surrendered my life to Him, none have been as rewarding as the smiles on the faces of my children. I'm beyond grateful that I've been blessed to give them the childhood I always knew they deserved. I'm not sure that they even realize how different our lives were just a couple of years ago.

I wasn't nearly as happy or hope-filled as I am now. I was so afraid of failure that I didn't expect anything from myself at all. I've had a revolutionary encounter with love that transformed my thinking. No longer am I chained to the notion that my insecurities exclude me from God's best. Instead I feel the authority of Christ dwelling in me. I thirst for the connection that I know will sustain me in my most stress-filled moments.

Did you ever feel stressed?

In spite of all the purpose on your life, did you ever feel like you needed to find that one secret place where everyone would simply leave you alone? I can't say for sure what homes looked like during your time, but I am pleased to inform you that nearly every home in America comes with a room designed specifically for the peace of mothers: a bathroom. It's not exactly the best-looking room in the house. It's also where we bathe, brush our teeth, and relieve our bodily functions, but most days I take what I can get. The peace the room offers isn't always a guarantee, but it's the closest I can get to a vacation every day, and it does the trick.

No longer am I chained to the notion that my insecurities exclude me from God's best.

It took about a year of training for each child, but I was able to teach my children proper bathroom etiquette. "When Mommy is in the bathroom, we do *not* force ourselves in," I explained to them. "Nod your head if you understand the words that are coming out of my mouth." Inevitably, it was only a day or two later that I had to have the exact same chat, but eventually they caught my drift. In many establishments, the bathroom is referred to as a restroom. I can't imagine a more fitting description, because outside of my bed, it's the only place in my life where I'm able to sneak a moment's rest.

Interestingly enough, I happen to think I may be turning into my mother. As children, my siblings and I graduated from a similar training on bathroom etiquette. Then she began making her restroom a bit of a sanctuary. At the most random times in the middle of the day, my siblings and I would search for my mother. We'd yell her name throughout the house repeatedly but never received an answer. After checking the garage to make sure her car was still parked at home, we would give up. It wasn't unusual for her to hide from us. She often went to great lengths to make sure that we couldn't find her. To this day I'm not exactly sure how many closets, restrooms, or pantries served as her hideaways, but I do know she managed *very* successfully to stay concealed. It became somewhat of a running joke in our household that our mother's bathroom had a secret passage that took her to a secret apartment.

If you're thinking that we could have just searched for our dad instead, then Joseph must have been a different type of father than mine. You see, there are some things only a mother can provide. My mother makes perfect hot breakfast cereal. She knows exactly how to cook the bacon and what shade to make the toast. When school projects were due, her creativity helped our work to trump whatever the other students brought in. Only my mother understood how to quickly stop the frequent nosebleeds I experienced. It's not that we couldn't ask Dad for help; it's just that we knew he'd end up asking Mom.

It's become comical that the very thing I once complained about as a child is now echoed in my children's whispering outside my bathroom door: "I think she's hiding from us!"

And they are right. I am intentionally and proudly following in the footsteps of my mother and hiding from my children.

I love them and all, but sometimes a mama just needs a break. Life can become so hectic at times that the only way to clear our heads is to take a moment to be still. Sometimes it feels as though I'm the only mother on the planet battling for her sanity. In carpool lines, all the other mothers look refreshed and ready to tackle the day. Most of the time I've peeled myself from my mattress, brushed my teeth with my eyes closed, and intentionally brushed my hair without looking in the mirror. I'm too afraid to see the bags under my eyes and the flyaways dominating my hair. I just need to make sure the kids get to school on time.

Life can become so hectic at times that the only way to clear our heads is to take a moment to be still.

I realize it's never kind to laugh at someone else's pain, but every now and then I see another mother just like me—a bit disheveled and obviously in need of another hour of sleep—and I smile. It's not one of those judgment smiles that I receive from the mothers in their workout clothes. It's not one of those pity smiles from the women in their business suits either. No, this smile is the one of a woman who knows what it's like to *need* a shot of energy in the morning in order to make it through the day.

Hardly a day has passed that I haven't felt the urge to call my mother to express my most sincere apology for the moments when she just needed one . . . two . . . three . . . or ten minutes to herself. She's now an empty nester, and when I share my sentiments of exhaustion with her, all she can do

166

is laugh. I'm assuming she's become so engrossed with her unlimited alone time that she has plenty of empathy but little to no sympathy for my plight.

I find comfort in the transparency of other women brave enough to admit they are tired. I believe that we can become so consumed with the facade of having it all together that we alienate other women into feeling they're alone in their stress. When I'm having one of those days when everything is going miraculously as planned, I try to document the process that allowed for the moments of success. Most of the time it comes down to proper planning, a full night's rest, and allowing my peace to set the tone for the day.

I'm also learning the power in the word *no*. To be honest, there would be many things on my calendar, and I wasn't exactly sure how they got there. As overextended as I felt, many of the tasks I needed to complete were favors I took on to help someone else. Eventually I'd taken on so many favors that I needed a favor myself. I needed to recognize when I was in over my head. I had to realize that sometimes the only relief I can offer a friend is a safe place to vent. I couldn't allow others' stress to be my demise. It's difficult enough to prioritize the many roles I am obligated to fill without taking on responsibilities I know that I can't truly handle.

Even with that revelation, there are many times I find myself still stretched a bit too thin to be the woman I envision in my head. I want to believe that somewhere in the minutes, hours, and days not documented in the Bible that you found a moment to nap, center yourself, and prepare for the possibilities of the next day. Feeling underappreciated by those we serve can add to our feelings of anxiety and stress.

We can't be of any good to anyone in our lives if we haven't had a moment to be good to ourselves. The only way to successfully give others our time, attention, and dedication is from the overflow of what we give ourselves. Too often we give from our already depleted souls and then have nothing left for us, let alone our relationship with God.

I searched all through the Scriptures for just a small hint of how you handled the many demands of your life. It was challenging to find a glimpse into your life until I realized Christ's life held the answer I'd been searching for all along. The book of Luke reveals that there were many times when Christ separated from the pack and withdrew to distant places so that He could pray. While His disciples waited for Him outside of the wilderness, Christ took a moment to reconnect with the source of His strength. He made His relationship with God His ultimate priority.

> *The only way to successfully give others our time, attention, and dedication is from the overflow of what we give ourselves.*

In Matthew 6:6 we're given instructions on how to maximize our alone time with God so that we can fully access the power of our relationship with Him. Once we've found our secret place where we are surrounded by stillness and quiet, we can open our hearts to Him: The focus will shift from you to God, and you will begin to sense His grace. It's so easy to begin to count on our own strength to get us through each day. The more that we are able to remove ourselves from the forefront of our minds and allow our focus to remain on God, the better we will understand that He's already given us grace to make it through the next day.

Even when we have difficulty taking care of our physical needs, we can't become so bogged down with our list of to-dos that we don't keep God first. As we make a conscious effort to seek Him first, we will recognize what He has given us the grace to finish and what weight we've placed on ourselves. We must trust that He holds our tomorrow in His hands and knows what struggle may await us the very next day. If he hasn't called us to bear it, it's not because we aren't capable of handling it, but rather because He's reserving our strength for His plan.

15

can we have a playdate?

Then Jesus came to them and said, "All authority in heaven and on earth has been given to me. Therefore go and make disciples of all nations, baptizing them in the name of the Father and of the Son and of the Holy Spirit, and teaching them to obey everything I have commanded you. And surely I am with you always, to the very end of the age."

Matthew 28:18–20

*D*ear Mary,

Last year for my son's eleventh birthday, he had only one item on his birthday list: money. At the time, he wasn't very interested in the latest fashion trends and didn't possess a notable affinity for video games. I must admit it was only a short time before that changed. But at eleven, Malachi was solely mesmerized by iconic creators like Walt Disney and Steve Jobs. He dreams of pursuing a career in the arts, but with creativity and innovation the world hasn't seen yet. He is confidently eclectic in his own skin. I wasn't surprised that he didn't really desire any material things for his birthday. When family and friends asked what other items to get him, I relayed his wishes. He had no intention of buying anything in particular because he considered the funds as saving for his future.

A week after his birthday, I received a call from his principal. I know most parents believe that their children have a heart of gold, but Malachi truly does! He's never been in trouble, and most teachers have a special place in their heart just for him. When I answered the call to speak with his principal, I wasn't really sure what to expect. She immediately eased my concern when she let me know he wasn't in trouble, nor had he been hurt. Malachi's principal went on to explain to me that a parent had come into her office to return $300 that Malachi had given another student. Evidently, upon hearing the student's father had lost his job, Malachi decided to give the girl his birthday money. While the principal and parent felt that it was kind, they didn't feel comfortable accepting the money from Malachi.

For his protection, I would have to have a discussion with Malachi about not carrying large sums of money with him to school, but I was proud of him. He was willing to offer what he could to help someone in need. Once we established the safety precautions, I took a moment to truly applaud the intention behind his giving. In a society where it can often be easy to believe that there are few genuinely good people left, my son had dispelled that myth. When I asked him what made him think to give his birthday money away, he reminded me of the times he's seen me give what cash we had in the car to someone in need. "Isn't that what we're supposed to do? Help as many people as we can?" he asked.

It instantly dawned on me that the power of being a Christian couldn't be weighed by the number of Scriptures we can recite or facts that we can memorize. Our ability to infuse the world with the love of Christ so that others may learn about the power of our God may be the greatest mission of all. What I've learned from your Son that sticks with me every moment of each day is that He did not just preach from the mountainside. He dared to touch the untouchable, speak to the outcasts, and be compassionate to those who hurt Him. He lived a life worth

Our ability to infuse the world with the love of Christ so that others may learn about the power of our God may be the greatest mission of all.

mimicking. When my son shared his birthday money with the family at his school, I realized that without even intending to, he'd allowed a family to have an encounter with God.

A contest of good versus evil has lasted throughout the ages. The strength to preserve our Light in the reality of much darkness is the hope of most believers. A growing number of people have chosen to stop believing in God because of the many calamities in the world. Often identifying themselves as atheist or agnostic, their questions to believers often begin with "If there is a God, how could he allow _____ to happen?" There have been many atrocities in the two thousand years since Christ left the earth. Acts of terrorism, senseless acts of murder, and a deteriorating trust in the goodness of humanity have inundated cultures and societies all around the world. Unanswered questions and unresolved hurt have created resentment in faith. It can be difficult to offer an answer that consoles the disbelief, but I do counter with another question that leaves them pondering. As many lives as we feel have been lost senselessly, how many have been saved divinely?

I can admit there have been many mornings I've awakened with air in my lungs and taken for granted that only God's grace allowed for it to happen. There have even been times when I didn't get what I wanted as quickly as I expected, and instead of being patient, I allowed my faith to be shaken. God's protection is so intricately woven in our lives that we don't always recognize it's constantly with us. We've been spared more times than we'll ever know, but we still allow our confusion to blind us to His ever-present grace.

For me, Christ represents the embodiment of my potential. His life is a reminder of the internal battle between the fallen humanity and the image of God in all of us. I am eternally grateful for the heavenly Father that sent us His Son, but I am also thankful for the humanity that made Him tangible for me. You were highly favored among women to give birth to Christ. Because He dwelled inside of you, I've been robbed of any excuse to become so downtrodden in life that I can no longer believe. He was accepted and rejected by people, wounded for our transgressions, tempted with pride, and fought fear, but He never lost focus on His Father.

God's protection is so intricately woven in our lives that we don't always recognize it's constantly with us.

I want to thank you for being so open to God that you allowed me to have an encounter with Him. Gabriel never mentioned to you the billions of lives that would be inspired to let God dwell inside of them. Thank you for teaching me that even the most unlikely candidate can be used to impact the world for God. I am a better mother, daughter, and sister because of the lessons I've learned about God through Christ. This world is a better place because of the world you created for Him. There may have been moments when you questioned whether or not your parenting was enough. I'm a living witness that your best was perfect for the life you were trusted to raise. You taught Him the courage to shine His light so that I could find my way and lead my children to God.

Conclusion

*D*ear Mothers,

It is my prayer that while you read this book, you realized you are not alone. I hope that there has been something written in this book that encourages you to recognize your children are in perfect hands. If this challenged you in any way to grow and become better, then do not waste time wondering if it's too late to fix the missteps you have made. Focus fully and intentionally on the task you have at hand. Whether you are at the beginning stages of motherhood, a few years in, or wondering if parenting will ever end, know that you have access to the strength and wisdom to build your children up. I've had the pleasure of encounters with mothers from all around the world. I have found it to be one of the universal languages of this world. There is no responsibility like molding a life in your hands. In time we learn the right amount of pressure to use and the delicate touch that only we can provide.

Don't compare your efforts with those of the other women in your life. Your observations of them are seeds that already exist in your life. You don't have to emulate them because they're already a part of you. All you have to do is just be! Trust that you have been appointed and selected because God believes you can bring out His best in your child. We cannot limit our teaching to the words that proceed from our mouths. Our lives must demonstrate the hopes that we believe exist inside of our children. If you give up on yourself, you'll teach them how to quit. Choose to believe that in spite of the duress you've faced, all things are working out for your good.

We cannot limit our teaching to the words that proceed from our mouths.

The life of Mary has been so significant for me because history reveals that she was a teenage mother. Certainly the times were much different then, and teen pregnancy didn't have the same stigma it does now. However, there was something about a young girl being trusted with life that made me want to examine how she was able to survive mental, emotional, and physical attacks. I imagined that once the news of God's impregnating her began to circulate, she was called crazy and made to become an outcast. There is no woman in the Bible more fitting to give insight on becoming a mother under extraordinary circumstances than Mary.

I'm not sure what mountains you'll have to climb in order to help your children see the bigger picture of developing and protecting their relationship with God. You may face many trials and withstand much adversity, but it can be done. Take rest in the truth that you've already won your battle because God is on your side.

Notes

Chapter 4: My Child Is Different

1. "Interview With Kate Davis," HBO Documentaries, http://www.hbo.com/documentaries/diagnosis-bipolar-five-families-search-for-answers/interview/kate-davis.html#/documentaries/diagnosis-bipolar-five-families-search-for-answers/interview/kate-davis.html.

2. Bipolar Disorder Health Center, "Bipolar Disorder Overview," WebMD, accessed April 30, 2015, http://www.webmd.com/bipolar-disorder/default.htm.

Chapter 5: I Didn't Make Dinner

1. "Global Christianity—A Report on the Size and Distribution of the World's Christian Population," Pew Research Center, December 19, 2011, http://www.pewforum.org/2011/12/19/global-christianity-exec/.

Chapter 8: They're My Do-Over

1. "Parenting styles," *Wikipedia*, last modified April 27, 2015, http://en.wikipedia.org/w/index.php?title=Parenting_styles&oldid=659574752.

2. Ibid.

Chapter 9: Too Hurt to Parent

1. David Hinckley, "Average American Watches 5 Hours of TV Per Day, Report Shows," *NY Daily News*, March 5, 2014, http://www.nydailynews.com/life-style/average-american-watches-5-hours-tv-day-article-1.1711954.

Chapter 10: I Need a Village

1. Eileen Keating, curator, "What Were Practice Apartments?" *From Domesticity to Modernity: What Was Home Economics?* online exhibit, Cornell University Library, Division of Rare and Manuscript Collections, accessed May 5, 2015, http://

rmc.library.cornell.edu/homeEc/cases/apartments.html. Also Desh Kapoor, "When Practice Babies Were Raised by Practice Mothers—Domecons, Norths, and Souths," Patheos.com, January 8, 2011, http://www.patheos.com/blogs/drishtikone/2011/01 /when-practice-babies-were-raised-practice-mothers-domecons-norths-and-souths/.

Chapter 11: Ends Don't Meet

1. "Poverty: 2013 Highlights," United States Census Bureau, accessed May 5, 2015, http://www.census.gov/hhes/www/poverty/about/overview/.

2. "2013 Poverty Guidelines," U.S. Department of Health and Human Services, accessed May 5, 2015, http://aspe.hhs.gov/poverty/13poverty.cfm.

Chapter 12: From Joy to Grief

1. Amy Robach, "Newtown Shooting: Couple Vow to Live for Dead Daughter Jessica Rekos," *Good Morning America*, ABCNews.com, December 17, 2012, http:// abcnews.go.com/US/newtown-shooting-couple-vow-live-dead-daughter-jessica/story ?id=17996306#.

2. Ibid.

3. "Miscarriage: Signs, Symptoms, Treatment and Prevention," American Pregnancy Association, last updated June 2014, http://americanpregnancy.org/pregnancy -complications/miscarriage/.

Sarah Jakes is a businesswoman, writer, speaker, and media personality. She is the senior editor of the online magazine *eMotions*, which is designed to educate and empower women. With her husband, Touré Roberts, she ministers to those in the TV, film, and music industries.

After graduating from high school at the age of sixteen in the top 10 of her class and in the top 10 percent of the nation, Sarah attended Texas Christian University, where she studied journalism. After a stint as an office liaison with the air force, Sarah joined the staff of TDJ Enterprises, where she was responsible for grassroots marketing efforts for the feature film *Not Easily Broken*. She then moved into a leadership role with the women's ministry at The Potter's House of Dallas, a multicultural, nondenominational church and humanitarian organization led by her parents, Bishop T. D. Jakes and Mrs. Serita Jakes. She also periodically served as host of *The Potter's Touch*, a daily inspirational broadcast airing on several national television networks.

Sarah blogs on love, life, family, and marriage and aspires to write articles and books that chronicle the lives of women who have overcome extreme challenges to reach their goals in life. Sarah details her personal journey in the memoir *Lost and Found* and offers encouragement for women in *Colliding With Destiny*.

When she is not pursuing her career endeavors, Sarah enjoys cooking, listening to music, and spending quality time with her husband and children. They make their home in the Los Angeles area. Connect with her online at sarahjakes.com.

More from Sarah Jakes!

Teenage pregnancy. Heartbreaking, high-profile divorce. A woman hurting and lost. With candid vulnerability and warmth, Sarah Jakes shares her inspiring story—and how she didn't let her pain dictate her future. Instead, she found herself surrounded by a God she'd given up on, crashing headlong with Him into a destiny she never could have imagined. Her story offers hope and encouragement to women of all ages. Perhaps you, like Sarah, find yourself wandering the detours of life. Regardless of how lost you feel, you, too, can be found.

Lost and Found

Perhaps you have a past you're struggling to overcome or circumstances that have kept you from being your true self. Despite your past pain, you can find redemption and restoration. Following the story of Ruth from the Old Testament, Sarah Jakes shows how, in the midst of loss, heartache, poverty, and shame, Ruth's most painful time became her most pivotal. Follow Ruth's life and discover the hope available to each of us. Your yesterday does not have to dictate your tomorrow.

Colliding With Destiny